©THE BOOK OF POWERSHELL

Copyrighted Material

THE BOOK OF POWER SHELL

AUTOMATION, SCRIPTING, AND REMOTE IT MANAGEMENT FOR WINDOWS

VICTOR P HENDERSON | ISSO-TECH ENTERPRISES™

CERTIFIED ETHICAL HACKER C|EH
ISSO-TECH PRESS™

VICTOR P HENDERSON | ISSO-TECH ENTERPRISES™

CERTIFIED ETHICAL HACKER C|EH
Copyrighted Material

THE BOOK OF POWER SHELL

AUTOMATION, SCRIPTING, AND REMOTE IT MANAGEMENT FOR WINDOWS

VICTOR P HENDERSON
CERTIFIED ETHICAL HACKER C|EH

ISSO-TECH ENTERPRISES

©THE BOOK OF POWERSHELL
Copyrighted Material

@ISSO.TECH.ENTERPRISES

©THE BOOK OF POWERSHELL

Copyrighted Material

THE BOOK OF POWER SHELL

AUTOMATION, SCRIPTING, AND REMOTE IT MANAGEMENT FOR WINDOWS

COPYRIGHT © 2024 BY VICTOR P HENDERSON
CERTIFIED ETHICAL HACKER C|EH

ISSO-TECH ENTERPRISES™

All rights reserved. The contents of this book, in whole or in part, are protected by copyright law. It is strictly prohibited to reproduce any parts thereof in any form; scanned, copied, uploaded, or stored in any retrieval system.

Distributed or transmitted in any form by any means-electronic, mechanical, photocopy, recording, or otherwise, without prior written permission is strictly prohibited without the author's explicit consent.

Unauthorized reproduction without the author's written permission constitutes theft of the author's intellectual property. Except for the use of brief quotations embodied in critical articles or reviews and certain other non-commercial uses as permitted by the United States Copyright Law and fair use.

Copyrighted Material
VICTOR P HENDERSON | ISSO-TECH ENTERPRISES™

CERTIFIED ETHICAL HACKER C|EH
ISSO-TECH PRESS™

VICTOR P HENDERSON | ISSO-TECH ENTERPRISES™

CERTIFIED ETHICAL HACKER C|EH
Copyrighted Material

For permission or other related inquiries, contact the author:
EMail: | PERMISSIONS@ISSOTECHENTERPRISES.COM
Web: | WWW.ISSOTECHENTERPRISES.COM
| WWW.ISSOTECH.COM
Social Media: @ISSO.TECH.ENTERPRISES

Written by: Victor P Henderson | Certified Ethical Hacker
ISSO-TECH ENTERPRISES™.
Published by: ISSO-TECH PRESS™

Thank you for respecting the author's rights.

Book and Cover Designed in Part By: **ISSO-TECH PRESS™**

©THE BOOK OF POWERSHELL
Copyrighted Material

@ISSO.TECH.ENTERPRISES

©THE BOOK OF POWERSHELL

Copyrighted Material

TABLE OF CONTENTS

Copyrighted Material
VICTOR P HENDERSON | ISSO-TECH ENTERPRISES™

CERTIFIED ETHICAL HACKER C|EH
ISSO-TECH PRESS™

VICTOR P HENDERSON | ISSO-TECH ENTERPRISES™

CERTIFIED ETHICAL HACKER C|EH
Copyrighted Material

THIS PAGE LEFT BLANK INTENTIONALLY!

©THE BOOK OF POWERSHELL
Copyrighted Material

@ISSO.TECH.ENTERPRISES

©THE BOOK OF POWERSHELL

Copyrighted Material

POWERSHELL

Copyrighted Material

VICTOR P HENDERSON | ISSO-TECH ENTERPRISES™

CERTIFIED ETHICAL HACKER C|EH

ISSO-TECH PRESS™

VICTOR P HENDERSON | ISSO-TECH ENTERPRISES™

CERTIFIED ETHICAL HACKER C|EH
Copyrighted Material

DISCLAIMER

The information presented in *The Book of PowerShell* is intended solely for educational and informational purposes. While every effort has been made to ensure that the content is accurate, comprehensive, and up-to-date, the author and publisher cannot guarantee that the techniques and strategies discussed in this book will work in every environment or situation. The material in this book is provided on an "as is" basis, without any warranties, either express or implied. The reader is responsible for determining the applicability of the information to their specific circumstances and for ensuring that it is used appropriately.

Given the complexity and variability of IT environments, the author and publisher strongly recommend that readers conduct thorough testing in a controlled setting before applying any procedures, configurations, or recommendations from this book to a live environment. The guidance provided in *The Book of PowerShell* is meant to serve as a general framework; however, individual results may vary based on factors such as network architecture, organizational policies, software versions, and user behavior.

The author and publisher expressly disclaim any liability for any direct, indirect, incidental, or consequential damages that may arise from the use or misuse of the information contained in this book. This includes, but is not limited to, data loss, security breaches, or operational disruptions. Readers are advised to consult with qualified professionals, including IT consultants, legal advisors,

©THE BOOK OF POWERSHELL
Copyrighted Material

@ISSO.TECH.ENTERPRISES

and cybersecurity experts, to obtain tailored advice and solutions that address the unique challenges of their specific environments.

Furthermore, this book is not intended to replace professional training, certification programs, or hands-on experience. While it serves as a valuable resource for gaining a deeper understanding of PowerShell, it should be used in conjunction with other learning tools and resources. The author encourages readers to continuously seek out additional knowledge and stay informed about the latest advancements in technology, security practices, and industry standards.

By using the information contained in *The Book of PowerShell*, you acknowledge that you have read, understood, and agreed to this disclaimer and that you accept full responsibility for any outcomes resulting from the application of the material provided. By viewing or reading this book, you hereby consent to this disclaimer and agree to its terms entirely.

Warning: The unauthorized reproduction or distribution of this copyrighted work is illegal. Criminal copyright infringement, including infringement without monetary gain, is investigated by the FBI and is punishable by up to five years in prison and a fine of $250,000.

Copyrighted Material
VICTOR P HENDERSON | ISSO-TECH ENTERPRISES™

CERTIFIED ETHICAL HACKER C|EH
ISSO-TECH PRESS™

229.320.151.8

VICTOR P HENDERSON | ISSO-TECH ENTERPRISES™

CERTIFIED ETHICAL HACKER C|EH
Copyrighted Material

THIS PAE LEFT BLANK INTENTIONALLY!

©THE BOOK OF POWERSHELL
Copyrighted Material

@ISSO.TECH.ENTERPRISES

©THE BOOK OF POWERSHELL

Copyrighted Material

POWERSHELL

Copyrighted Material

VICTOR P HENDERSON | ISSO-TECH ENTERPRISES™

CERTIFIED ETHICAL HACKER C|EH

ISSO-TECH PRESS™

INTRODUCTION

Welcome to *The Book of PowerShell*, a comprehensive guide designed to empower IT professionals and enthusiasts with the knowledge and skills needed to harness the full potential of PowerShell. As a powerful scripting language and command-line shell, PowerShell is an indispensable tool in modern IT environments, enabling users to automate complex tasks, manage system configurations, and streamline administrative processes with unparalleled efficiency.

In this book, we embark on an in-depth exploration of PowerShell, providing both foundational principles and advanced techniques. Whether you are a novice looking to build a solid understanding or an experienced professional seeking to refine your expertise, this guide offers valuable insights and practical examples tailored to various levels of proficiency.

We begin by laying a strong foundation with the core concepts and fundamental commands that form the bedrock of PowerShell scripting. From there, we delve into more sophisticated topics, including script writing, module development, and integration with other technologies. Each chapter is crafted to build upon the previous one, ensuring a coherent and progressive learning experience.

Throughout *The Book of PowerShell*, you will find real-world scenarios and hands-on exercises designed to reinforce your understanding and help you apply the concepts in practical

©THE BOOK OF POWERSHELL
Copyrighted Material

@ISSO.TECH.ENTERPRISES

Copyrighted Material

situations. Our aim is to equip you with the tools and confidence to tackle challenges, optimize workflows, and drive efficiency in your IT operations.

In addition to technical knowledge, this book emphasizes best practices and effective strategies for leveraging PowerShell in diverse environments. We address common pitfalls, offer troubleshooting tips, and provide guidance on maintaining security and compliance while utilizing PowerShell.

As technology continues to evolve, staying current with new developments and techniques is essential. This book serves not only as a learning resource but also as a reference guide that you can return to as you advance in your PowerShell journey. Our goal is to support your growth and success in mastering PowerShell and making a meaningful impact in your professional endeavors.

Thank you for choosing *The Book of PowerShell*. We invite you to dive into the pages that follow, embrace the challenges, and unlock the full capabilities of PowerShell. Your journey toward becoming a proficient PowerShell user begins here.

INTRODUCTION

Copyrighted Material
VICTOR P HENDERSON | ISSO-TECH ENTERPRISES™

CERTIFIED ETHICAL HACKER C|EH
ISSO-TECH PRESS™

229.320.151.8

VICTOR P HENDERSON | ISSO-TECH ENTERPRISES™

CERTIFIED ETHICAL HACKER C|EH
Copyrighted Material

THIS [AGE LEFT BLANK INTENTIONALLY!

©THE BOOK OF POWERSHELL
Copyrighted Material

@ISSO.TECH.ENTERPRISES

©THE BOOK OF POWERSHELL

Copyrighted Material

POWERSHELL

Copyrighted Material

VICTOR P HENDERSON | ISSO-TECH ENTERPRISES™

CERTIFIED ETHICAL HACKER C|EH

ISSO-TECH PRESS™

VICTOR P HENDERSON | ISSO-TECH ENTERPRISES™

CERTIFIED ETHICAL HACKER C|EH
Copyrighted Material

EPIGRAPH

©THE BOOK OF POWERSHELL
Copyrighted Material

@ISSO.TECH.ENTERPRISES

©THE BOOK OF POWERSHELL

Copyrighted Material

EPIGRAPH | THE BOOK OF POWERSHELL
ISSO-TECH ENTERPRISES™

"Technology is best when it brings people together. PowerShell is more than just a scripting language; it is a bridge that connects the complexities of IT management with the simplicity of automation, transforming the way we interact with systems and solve problems."

- VICTOR P HENDERSON -
CERTIFIED ETHICAL HACKER C|EH

ISSO-TECH ENTERPRISES

Copyrighted Material
VICTOR P HENDERSON | ISSO-TECH ENTERPRISES™

CERTIFIED ETHICAL HACKER C|EH
ISSO-TECH PRESS™

VICTOR P HENDERSON | ISSO-TECH ENTERPRISES™

CERTIFIED ETHICAL HACKER C|EH
Copyrighted Material

THIS PAGE LEFT BLANK INTENTIONALLY!

©THE BOOK OF POWERSHELL
Copyrighted Material

④ISSO.TECH.ENTERPRISES

©THE BOOK OF POWERSHELL

Copyrighted Material

POWERSHELL

Copyrighted Material

VICTOR P HENDERSON | ISSO-TECH ENTERPRISES™

CERTIFIED ETHICAL HACKER C|EH

ISSO-TECH PRESS™

VICTOR P HENDERSON | ISSO-TECH ENTERPRISES™

CERTIFIED ETHICAL HACKER C|EH
Copyrighted Material

POWERSHELL

©THE BOOK OF POWERSHELL

Copyrighted Material

@ISSO.TECH.ENTERPRISES

Copyrighted Material

POWERSHELL | THE HISTORY
TECHNOLOGY AUTOMATION

The technology purpose of PowerShell is to provide a comprehensive framework for automating tasks, managing systems, and configuring environments. Here's a detailed breakdown of its primary purposes:

1. Automation and Scripting

PowerShell enables users to automate repetitive tasks and create scripts to handle complex workflows. By writing and executing PowerShell scripts, administrators and developers can automate tasks such as system updates, user management, data processing, and configuration changes.

2. Configuration Management

PowerShell offers tools for configuring and managing system settings, applications, and services. This includes the ability to manage Windows features, network settings, and application configurations. It also supports Desired State Configuration (DSC), a feature that ensures systems remain in a desired configuration state.

3. System Administration

PowerShell provides a unified interface for managing and administering various aspects of the operating system. It can handle tasks such as user account management, file system

Copyrighted Material
VICTOR P HENDERSON | ISSO-TECH ENTERPRISES™

CERTIFIED ETHICAL HACKER C|EH
ISSO-TECH PRESS™

229.320.151.8

operations, process monitoring, and service management. This helps system administrators streamline their workflows and maintain system stability.

4. Integration with Other Technologies

PowerShell integrates with a wide range of technologies and platforms, including Windows, Azure, SQL Server, Exchange, and more. This integration allows users to manage and automate tasks across different systems and services using a consistent scripting environment.

5. Data Manipulation and Reporting

PowerShell includes powerful cmdlets for working with data, such as importing, exporting, and manipulating data from files, databases, and other sources. This makes it a valuable tool for generating reports, analyzing data, and performing data-driven tasks.

6. Remote Management

PowerShell supports remote management capabilities, allowing users to run commands and scripts on remote systems. This feature is essential for managing multiple servers or workstations from a central location, enabling efficient administration of large-scale environments.

7. Extensibility and Customization

©THE BOOK OF POWERSHELL
Copyrighted Material

@ISSO.TECH.ENTERPRISES

Copyrighted Material

PowerShell is highly extensible, allowing users to create custom cmdlets, modules, and scripts to extend its functionality. This flexibility enables users to tailor PowerShell to meet specific needs and integrate it with other tools and systems.

8. Cross-Platform Support

With the introduction of PowerShell Core (now simply PowerShell), the framework extends its capabilities to non-Windows platforms, including macOS and Linux. This cross-platform support facilitates automation and management tasks across diverse operating environments.

9. Security and Compliance

PowerShell includes features for managing security settings, enforcing compliance policies, and monitoring system activity. It helps ensure that systems adhere to security standards and regulatory requirements by automating security-related tasks and auditing.

In summary, the technology purpose of PowerShell is to provide a versatile, powerful, and unified scripting environment that enhances the efficiency and effectiveness of IT management, system administration, and automation across various platforms and technologies.

Copyrighted Material
VICTOR P HENDERSON | ISSO-TECH ENTERPRISES™

CERTIFIED ETHICAL HACKER C|EH
ISSO-TECH PRESS™

229.320.151.8

Origins and Development: PowerShell, initially known as "Monad," was developed by Microsoft as a task automation and configuration management framework. Its development began in the early 2000s, spearheaded by Jeffrey Snover, a Microsoft engineer who sought to address the limitations of existing scripting tools like the Windows Script Host (WSH) and Command Prompt. The goal was to create a powerful, versatile scripting language that could integrate deeply with the Windows operating system and provide a more comprehensive automation solution.

Initial Release: PowerShell was first released as "Windows PowerShell" in November 2006, as part of the Windows Server 2008 and Windows Vista operating systems. This initial version, PowerShell 1.0, introduced a new command-line shell and scripting language, featuring cmdlets (command-lets), a robust object-oriented framework, and a consistent syntax for managing various system components.

Evolution and Expansion: The subsequent versions of PowerShell built upon its core features, enhancing its capabilities and expanding its reach:

- **PowerShell 2.0 (2009):** Released with Windows 7 and Windows Server 2008 R2, this version introduced advanced features such as the Integrated Scripting Environment (ISE), remote management capabilities, and new cmdlets for improved functionality.
- **PowerShell 3.0 (2012):** Bundled with Windows 8 and Windows Server 2012, this version brought significant improvements, including workflow support, enhanced

©**THE BOOK OF POWERSHELL**
Copyrighted Material

④ISSO.TECH.ENTERPRISES

Copyrighted Material

debugging, and additional cmdlets for managing and automating tasks.

- **PowerShell 4.0 (2013):** Released alongside Windows 8.1 and Windows Server 2012 R2, PowerShell 4.0 introduced Desired State Configuration (DSC), a powerful feature for managing configuration consistency across systems.
- **PowerShell 5.0 (2016):** Included with Windows 10 and Windows Server 2016, this version introduced new features such as enhanced security, improved debugging, and additional cmdlets for managing modern environments.

Open Source and Cross-Platform: In August 2016, Microsoft announced the open-sourcing of PowerShell, which led to the creation of "PowerShell Core." PowerShell Core, based on the .NET Core framework, extends the capabilities of PowerShell to non-Windows platforms, including macOS and Linux. This move marked a significant shift, making PowerShell a versatile tool for cross-platform automation and management.

Modern Developments:

- **PowerShell 6.x (2018):** The first release of PowerShell Core, featuring cross-platform support and improvements in performance and compatibility.
- **PowerShell 7.x (2020–present):** Rebranded as simply "PowerShell," these versions build upon the legacy of PowerShell Core, integrating new features, bug fixes, and improvements while maintaining cross-platform support.

Copyrighted Material
VICTOR P HENDERSON | ISSO-TECH ENTERPRISES™

CERTIFIED ETHICAL HACKER C|EH
ISSO-TECH PRESS™

Impact and Adoption: PowerShell has become a widely adopted tool in IT environments, known for its powerful scripting capabilities, automation potential, and integration with various Microsoft products and services. Its extensibility, support for complex workflows, and robust community contributions have cemented its position as a critical tool for system administrators, developers, and IT professionals.

©THE BOOK OF POWERSHELL

Copyrighted Material

THIS PAGE LEFT BLANK INTENTIONALLY!

POWERSHELL

Copyrighted Material

VICTOR P HENDERSON | ISSO-TECH ENTERPRISES™

CERTIFIED ETHICAL HACKER C|EH

ISSO-TECH PRESS™

VICTOR P HENDERSON | ISSO-TECH ENTERPRISES™

CERTIFIED ETHICAL HACKER C|EH
Copyrighted Material

SPECIAL THANKS

I would like to extend my deepest gratitude to the many individuals and organizations whose support, expertise, and encouragement have been instrumental in bringing this book to life.

To My Wife: Your unwavering belief in my abilities has been a source of constant motivation. Your love, patience, and understanding have been the foundation upon which all my successes are built.

To My Mentors and Colleagues: Your guidance, insights, and shared knowledge have been invaluable. I am deeply thankful for the opportunities to learn from your experiences, and I appreciate the collaborative spirit that has enriched this work.

To the IT Community: This book is a reflection of the collective wisdom and innovation that define our field. I am grateful to the many professionals, educators, and industry leaders whose contributions have shaped the landscape of Information Technology.

To the Readers and Aspiring Technologists: Your passion for learning and desire to push the boundaries of what is possible inspire me. It is my hope that this book serves as a valuable resource on your journey to mastering the complexities of technology.

©THE BOOK OF POWERSHELL
Copyrighted Material

@ISSO.TECH.ENTERPRISES

Copyrighted Material

To ISSO-TECH ENTERPRISES Team: Your dedication and hard work have been crucial in making this project a reality. Your commitment to excellence, creativity, and technical expertise has been a driving force behind the success of this endeavor.

To My Publishers and Editors at ISSO-TECH PRESS: Thank you for your professionalism, attention to detail, and tireless efforts to ensure this book meets the highest standards. Your partnership has been a cornerstone of this journey.

To My Friends and Supporters: Your encouragement and belief in my vision have provided the fuel necessary to complete this project. I am forever grateful for your support and friendship.

Finally, to all those who have walked this path with me, both named and unnamed, your contributions have not gone unnoticed. This book is a testament to the power of collaboration, perseverance, and the shared pursuit of knowledge. Thank you.

Copyrighted Material
VICTOR P HENDERSON | ISSO-TECH ENTERPRISES™

CERTIFIED ETHICAL HACKER C|EH
ISSO-TECH PRESS™

VICTOR P HENDERSON | ISSO-TECH ENTERPRISES™

CERTIFIED ETHICAL HACKER C|EH
Copyrighted Material

THIS PAGE LEFT BLANK INTENTIONALLY!

©THE BOOK OF POWERSHELL
Copyrighted Material

@ISSO.TECH.ENTERPRISES

Copyrighted Material

POWERSHELL

Copyrighted Material

VICTOR P HENDERSON | ISSO-TECH ENTERPRISES™

CERTIFIED ETHICAL HACKER C|EH
ISSO-TECH PRESS™

VICTOR P HENDERSON | ISSO-TECH ENTERPRISES™

CERTIFIED ETHICAL HACKER C|EH

Copyrighted Material

DEDICATION

THIS BOOK IS DEDICATED IN THE LOVING MEMORY OF MY MOTHER

©THE BOOK OF POWERSHELL

Copyrighted Material

@ISSO.TECH.ENTERPRISES

©THE BOOK OF POWERSHELL

Copyrighted Material

POWERSHELL

Copyrighted Material

VICTOR P HENDERSON | ISSO-TECH ENTERPRISES™

CERTIFIED ETHICAL HACKER C|EH

ISSO-TECH PRESS™

VICTOR P HENDERSON | ISSO-TECH ENTERPRISES™

CERTIFIED ETHICAL HACKER C|EH
Copyrighted Material

CHAPTER 1
POWERSHELL
MANAGEMENT

©THE BOOK OF POWERSHELL
Copyrighted Material

@ISSO.TECH.ENTERPRISES

Copyrighted Material

CHAPTER 1 | POWERSHELL
NETWORK MANAGEMENT

The Role of PowerShell in Small Business IT

The integration of PowerShell into small business IT infrastructures has become essential for enhancing operational efficiency and streamlining various management tasks. As small businesses often operate with limited resources, the ability to automate routine processes becomes a game-changer. PowerShell, a powerful scripting language and command-line shell, provides IT professionals, system administrators, and network engineers with the tools necessary to automate repetitive tasks, manage systems, and improve overall productivity. By leveraging PowerShell, small businesses can effectively manage their IT resources, ensuring that their systems are running smoothly and securely.

One of the most significant advantages of PowerShell is its versatility in managing a diverse range of IT environments. From on-premises servers to cloud-based solutions such as Azure and AWS, PowerShell enables IT professionals to interact with different platforms seamlessly. This capability is particularly crucial for small businesses that may not have the luxury of dedicated teams for each technology stack. With PowerShell, tasks such as user account management, system updates, and resource provisioning can be executed through scripts, reducing the time and effort required for manual intervention.

Copyrighted Material
VICTOR P HENDERSON | ISSO-TECH ENTERPRISES™

CERTIFIED ETHICAL HACKER C|EH
ISSO-TECH PRESS™

PowerShell's role in security and compliance cannot be overstated, especially in an era where data breaches and regulatory requirements are at the forefront of business concerns. By utilizing PowerShell scripts, small businesses can implement security best practices, automate compliance checks, and generate detailed reports for audits. For instance, IT administrators can create scripts that regularly assess system configurations and user permissions, ensuring that any deviations from established security policies are promptly addressed. This proactive approach not only safeguards sensitive data but also helps maintain compliance with industry regulations.

In addition to security, PowerShell plays a vital role in database management and DevOps integration for small businesses. As organizations increasingly rely on data-driven decision-making, the ability to automate database operations such as backups, maintenance, and performance monitoring becomes crucial. PowerShell provides an efficient means to manage databases, allowing system administrators to execute complex queries and automate routine tasks effortlessly. Furthermore, in the context of DevOps, PowerShell facilitates seamless integration between development and operations, enabling teams to deploy applications faster and more reliably.

Lastly, embracing PowerShell in IT support and troubleshooting practices can significantly enhance the service delivery capabilities of small businesses. The ability to quickly diagnose issues and execute fixes through scripting not only improves response times but also reduces downtime. IT professionals can utilize PowerShell to gather system information, analyze logs, and deploy solutions across multiple devices from a single console. This centralized

©THE BOOK OF POWERSHELL
Copyrighted Material

@ISSO.TECH.ENTERPRISES

Copyrighted Material

approach to troubleshooting ensures that small businesses can maintain high levels of service availability, ultimately leading to improved customer satisfaction and business success. As small businesses continue to evolve in the digital landscape, PowerShell will remain a critical component in their IT strategy, driving efficiency and innovation.

Copyrighted Material
VICTOR P HENDERSON | ISSO-TECH ENTERPRISES™

CERTIFIED ETHICAL HACKER C|EH
ISSO-TECH PRESS™

Overview of Network Management

Effective network management is a critical component for the success of small businesses, where the reliability and performance of IT infrastructure directly influence productivity and customer satisfaction. In an era where digital transformation is accelerating, small businesses must adopt robust network management strategies to ensure seamless operations. This involves not only monitoring and maintaining network performance but also implementing proactive measures to prevent issues before they impact business operations. The integration of PowerShell into network management practices provides a powerful avenue for system administrators and IT professionals to automate tasks, enhance efficiency, and improve overall network health.

PowerShell offers a versatile scripting environment that enables network engineers to streamline routine tasks such as configuration management, performance monitoring, and troubleshooting. By leveraging PowerShell's capabilities, IT professionals can create scripts that automate repetitive processes, reducing the time spent on manual interventions. Additionally, PowerShell's compatibility with various network devices and systems makes it an essential tool for network management in diverse environments. This flexibility is particularly beneficial for small businesses that may not have the resources to maintain a large IT team, allowing them to operate more efficiently with limited personnel.

Monitoring network performance is paramount for identifying potential bottlenecks and ensuring optimal functionality. PowerShell scripts can be employed to gather real-time data regarding bandwidth usage, device health, and network latency,

©THE BOOK OF POWERSHELL
Copyrighted Material

@ISSO.TECH.ENTERPRISES

Copyrighted Material

allowing for timely responses to emerging issues. Furthermore, the ability to visualize this data through dashboards enhances decision-making capabilities for IT professionals. By utilizing PowerShell in conjunction with other monitoring tools, small businesses can gain insights into their network performance, thus enabling them to make informed investments in their IT infrastructure.

Security and compliance are other critical aspects of network management that small businesses must prioritize. With the increasing frequency of cyber threats, it is essential to implement robust security measures to protect sensitive data. PowerShell can be instrumental in enforcing security protocols, automating compliance checks, and conducting vulnerability assessments. By integrating PowerShell scripts into their security frameworks, IT professionals can ensure that their networks are resilient against potential attacks while maintaining compliance with industry standards and regulations.

In conclusion, effective network management is vital for small businesses seeking to enhance their operational efficiency and security posture. PowerShell serves as a key enabler in this domain, providing IT professionals with the tools needed to automate tasks, monitor performance, and enforce security measures. As small businesses continue to navigate the complexities of the digital landscape, mastering PowerShell for network management will be a strategic advantage, allowing them to leverage technology for sustained growth and success.

Copyrighted Material

VICTOR P HENDERSON | ISSO-TECH ENTERPRISES™

CERTIFIED ETHICAL HACKER C|EH
ISSO-TECH PRESS™

Benefits of Using PowerShell for Network Management

In today's fast-paced digital landscape, small businesses increasingly rely on efficient network management to maintain operational integrity and enhance productivity. PowerShell, a powerful scripting language and command-line shell, offers a versatile solution tailored for IT professionals, system administrators, and network engineers. By leveraging PowerShell, organizations can streamline network management tasks, automate repetitive processes, and ensure compliance with industry standards, ultimately driving business success.

One of the primary benefits of using PowerShell for network management is its ability to automate routine tasks. Small businesses often face limited resources and personnel constraints, making it imperative to maximize efficiency. PowerShell allows for the scripting of repetitive tasks such as user account management, network configuration, and system monitoring. With automation, IT teams can reduce manual errors, save time, and focus on more strategic initiatives that align with business goals. This capability not only enhances productivity but also ensures that network operations are more reliable and consistent.

PowerShell's extensive integration capabilities further enhance its value for network management. It can seamlessly connect with various systems and applications, including cloud services like Azure and AWS, allowing businesses to manage hybrid environments effectively. This integration enables administrators to execute commands across different platforms, providing a unified approach to network management. Additionally, PowerShell supports API interactions, empowering small

©**THE BOOK OF POWERSHELL**
Copyrighted Material

Copyrighted Material

businesses to customize their network solutions, thus improving service delivery and operational flexibility.

Security and compliance are critical considerations for any organization, especially for small businesses that may not have dedicated security teams. PowerShell offers robust features for managing security policies and compliance requirements. With its built-in cmdlets and scripting capabilities, IT professionals can implement security configurations, monitor compliance status, and generate reports to demonstrate adherence to regulatory standards. This proactive approach to security not only protects sensitive data but also builds trust with clients and stakeholders.

Finally, the community and support surrounding PowerShell provide an invaluable resource for IT professionals and network engineers. The wealth of online forums, tutorials, and documentation allows users to share best practices, troubleshoot issues, and refine their skills. For small businesses, this collaborative environment fosters continuous learning and adaptation in an ever-evolving tech landscape. By mastering PowerShell, IT teams can stay ahead of emerging trends, leverage advanced techniques, and ultimately ensure their network management strategies are both effective and sustainable.

Copyrighted Material

VICTOR P HENDERSON | ISSO-TECH ENTERPRISES™

CERTIFIED ETHICAL HACKER C|EH
ISSO-TECH PRESS™

VICTOR P HENDERSON | ISSO-TECH ENTERPRISES™

CERTIFIED ETHICAL HACKER C|EH
Copyrighted Material

©THE BOOK OF POWERSHELL
Copyrighted Material

@ISSO.TECH.ENTERPRISES

Copyrighted Material

POWERSHELL

Copyrighted Material

VICTOR P HENDERSON | ISSO-TECH ENTERPRISES™

CERTIFIED ETHICAL HACKER C|EH

ISSO-TECH PRESS™

229.320.151.8

CHAPTER 2
GETTING STARTED

©THE BOOK OF POWERSHELL
Copyrighted Material

@ISSO.TECH.ENTERPRISES

CHAPTER 2 | GETTING STARTED
INSTALLATION & CONFIGURATION

Installing PowerShell

Installing PowerShell is a crucial step for small businesses and IT professionals aiming to streamline network management and automate routine tasks. PowerShell, a powerful automation and configuration management framework, provides a command-line shell and scripting language that is essential for system administrators, network engineers, and anyone involved in IT operations. This chapter will guide you through the various installation methods available for PowerShell, ensuring that you can get started quickly and efficiently.

First, it is important to note that PowerShell is available on various platforms, including Windows, macOS, and Linux. For Windows users, PowerShell comes pre-installed with most versions of the operating system starting from Windows 7. However, to leverage the latest features and improvements, it is recommended to install the latest version of PowerShell Core, which is cross-platform. You can download the installer directly from the official PowerShell GitHub repository, where you will find detailed instructions for installation on each supported platform, ensuring you are equipped with the most current tools for your automation and network management tasks.

For macOS and Linux users, installing PowerShell Core requires a few additional steps compared to the Windows installation. The

Copyrighted Material
VICTOR P HENDERSON | ISSO-TECH ENTERPRISES™

CERTIFIED ETHICAL HACKER C|EH
ISSO-TECH PRESS™

installation process typically involves using package managers such as Homebrew for macOS or APT and YUM for various Linux distributions. Each package manager has its own set of commands, which are clearly outlined in the official documentation. Following these instructions will help you set up PowerShell on non-Windows systems, allowing for seamless integration into cross-platform environments, which is increasingly common in modern IT practices.

Once you have successfully installed PowerShell, it is advisable to familiarize yourself with the environment. Launch PowerShell and explore its features, such as the integrated scripting environment (ISE) and the command-line interface that supports cmdlets designed for network management. You can also customize your environment by installing useful modules that extend PowerShell's functionality. For example, modules specific to Azure or AWS can facilitate cloud management, while others can assist in security and compliance tasks, enhancing your overall IT management strategy.

Finally, as you embark on your journey with PowerShell, consider investing time in learning best practices for scripting and automation. Understanding how to write efficient scripts and utilize PowerShell's advanced features can significantly improve your operational efficiency. There are numerous resources available, including online courses, documentation, and community forums, where you can deepen your knowledge and connect with other professionals. By mastering PowerShell, you empower your small business with the capability to automate processes, manage networks effectively, and respond to IT challenges with agility and confidence.

©THE BOOK OF POWERSHELL
Copyrighted Material

⒜ISSO.TECH.ENTERPRISES

©THE BOOK OF POWERSHELL

Copyrighted Material

Copyrighted Material

VICTOR P HENDERSON | ISSO-TECH ENTERPRISES™

CERTIFIED ETHICAL HACKER C|EH

ISSO-TECH PRESS™

VICTOR P HENDERSON | ISSO-TECH ENTERPRISES™

CERTIFIED ETHICAL HACKER C|EH
Copyrighted Material

Understanding PowerShell Syntax

Understanding PowerShell syntax is crucial for small businesses and IT professionals aiming to leverage this powerful scripting language for network management and automation. PowerShell syntax is designed to be intuitive and user-friendly, making it easier for system administrators and network engineers to script solutions that optimize their environments. By familiarizing oneself with the key components of PowerShell syntax, users can effectively harness the full potential of PowerShell to streamline tasks, enhance productivity, and maintain robust network systems.

At the core of PowerShell syntax are cmdlets, which are built-in functions that perform specific tasks. A cmdlet typically follows a verb-noun format, such as `Get-Process` or `Set-Item`, which allows users to quickly understand their purpose. This standardized naming convention not only enhances readability but also aids in discovering available commands through tab completion and the Get-Command cmdlet. For small businesses, this means less time spent searching for commands and more time focused on implementing effective solutions tailored to their unique needs.

PowerShell's pipeline feature is another essential aspect of its syntax. The pipeline allows users to pass the output of one cmdlet as the input to another, enabling the creation of complex operations in a streamlined manner. For IT professionals, mastering the pipeline is vital for developing efficient scripts that minimize redundancy and leverage data transformation. By chaining cmdlets together, system administrators can automate multiple tasks, such as retrieving system information and filtering results, thus reducing manual effort and increasing accuracy in daily operations.

©THE BOOK OF POWERSHELL
Copyrighted Material

④ISSO.TECH.ENTERPRISES

Additionally, understanding PowerShell's data types and objects is fundamental for effective scripting. PowerShell is built on the .NET framework, allowing it to treat everything as an object, from strings to complex data structures. This object-oriented approach enables users to manipulate data with ease, making it particularly useful for tasks such as database management and cloud resource manipulation. For network engineers, this means that operations such as querying Active Directory or managing Azure resources can be performed with greater precision, ultimately leading to improved system performance and reliability.

In summary, a solid grasp of PowerShell syntax is indispensable for small businesses and IT professionals looking to harness its capabilities for network management and automation. By understanding cmdlets, leveraging the pipeline, and utilizing PowerShell's object-oriented nature, users can develop scripts that not only streamline operations but also enhance overall efficiency and compliance. As organizations increasingly turn to PowerShell for tasks ranging from DevOps integration to security auditing, mastering its syntax will provide a competitive edge in today's technology-driven landscape.

Copyrighted Material
VICTOR P HENDERSON | ISSO-TECH ENTERPRISES™

CERTIFIED ETHICAL HACKER C|EH
ISSO-TECH PRESS™

Basic Cmdlets for Network Management

In the realm of network management, PowerShell offers a robust set of cmdlets that empower small businesses, IT professionals, system administrators, and network engineers to efficiently monitor and manage their network infrastructure. Understanding these basic cmdlets is essential for effectively harnessing PowerShell's capabilities for automation and troubleshooting. This subchapter will introduce key cmdlets that serve as the foundation for network management tasks, providing a stepping stone for more advanced operations and scripts.

One of the primary cmdlets used for network management is `Get-NetIPAddress`. This cmdlet retrieves the IP address configuration for all network interfaces on a local or remote machine. By utilizing this cmdlet, administrators can quickly assess the IP settings of their network devices, including IP address, subnet mask, and default gateway. This capability is particularly beneficial for small businesses that may lack extensive IT resources, allowing them to manage their network configurations with ease. Additionally, filtering options can help isolate specific interfaces or configurations, streamlining the troubleshooting process.

Another essential cmdlet is `Test-Connection`, which functions similarly to the traditional ping command. This cmdlet tests the connectivity between the local computer and a specified remote host. It is invaluable for diagnosing network issues, as it can verify whether a device is reachable and measure response times. For small businesses, regular connectivity tests can preemptively identify potential network problems, ensuring that any disruptions are addressed before they impact operations. The flexibility of `Test-Connection` allows for options such as specifying the number of pings or adjusting timeouts, thus providing tailored testing scenarios.

For managing network shares, the `Get-SmbShare` cmdlet plays a crucial role. It retrieves information about shared folders on a network, including their names, paths, and access permissions. This cmdlet is particularly useful for system administrators who need to maintain file sharing across their organization. By understanding the shares that exist on their network, businesses can enforce security policies, audit access rights, and ensure compliance with data management practices. Moreover, combining `Get-SmbShare` with other cmdlets can facilitate the automation of share management tasks, enhancing overall efficiency.

Lastly, the `Get-NetRoute` cmdlet is instrumental in viewing the routing table of a network device. It provides insights into how data packets are directed within the network, which is essential for troubleshooting routing issues or optimizing network performance. By analyzing the output of `Get-NetRoute`, administrators can identify misconfigurations or conflicts that may hinder connectivity. For small businesses, having the ability to effectively manage routing information can significantly improve their network reliability and performance, fostering a more responsive and resilient IT environment.

In conclusion, mastering these fundamental cmdlets lays the groundwork for effective network management using PowerShell.

Copyrighted Material
VICTOR P HENDERSON | ISSO-TECH ENTERPRISES™

CERTIFIED ETHICAL HACKER C|EH
ISSO-TECH PRESS™

VICTOR P HENDERSON | ISSO-TECH ENTERPRISES™

CERTIFIED ETHICAL HACKER C|EH
Copyrighted Material

As small businesses and IT professionals delve deeper into PowerShell scripting, they will find that these basic tools can be integrated into more complex workflows and automated processes. By leveraging these cmdlets, organizations can enhance their network management capabilities, ensuring that their IT infrastructure remains efficient, secure, and compliant with industry standards.

©THE BOOK OF POWERSHELL
Copyrighted Material

@ISSO.TECH.ENTERPRISES

Copyrighted Material

POWERSHELL

Copyrighted Material

VICTOR P HENDERSON | ISSO-TECH ENTERPRISES™

CERTIFIED ETHICAL HACKER C|EH

ISSO-TECH PRESS™

VICTOR P HENDERSON | ISSO-TECH ENTERPRISES™

CERTIFIED ETHICAL HACKER C|EH
Copyrighted Material

CHAPTER 3
FUNDAMENTALS FOR NETWORK ENGINEERS

©THE BOOK OF POWERSHELL
Copyrighted Material

@ISSO.TECH.ENTERPRISES

Copyrighted Material

CHAPTER 3 | FUNDAMENTALS
SKILLES NETWORK ENGINEERS

Working with Variables and Data Types

Working with Variables and Data Types

In PowerShell, variables serve as essential building blocks for scripting and automation, particularly for small businesses looking to streamline their network management tasks. A variable in PowerShell is essentially a storage location identified by a name, allowing administrators to store and manipulate data efficiently. By understanding how to declare and utilize variables, IT professionals can create scripts that dynamically respond to changing conditions in their network environments. This flexibility is crucial for managing resources effectively, whether it be in local infrastructures or cloud-based solutions like Azure and AWS.

PowerShell supports several data types, each designed to handle specific kinds of data. Common data types include strings for text, integers for whole numbers, and booleans for true/false values. Additionally, PowerShell offers more complex types such as arrays and hashtables that can hold collections of items. Understanding these data types is vital for system administrators and network engineers, as it allows them to optimize their scripts for performance and accuracy. For instance, when working with large datasets or integrating with APIs, choosing the appropriate data type can significantly impact the efficiency of the operation.

Copyrighted Material
VICTOR P HENDERSON | ISSO-TECH ENTERPRISES™

CERTIFIED ETHICAL HACKER C|EH
ISSO-TECH PRESS™

When declaring variables in PowerShell, the syntax is straightforward: simply use the dollar sign followed by the variable name. It is good practice to create meaningful variable names that clearly describe the data they hold. This not only improves the readability of scripts but also facilitates collaboration among team members who may need to maintain or modify the code later. For small businesses with limited IT resources, maintaining clarity and simplicity in scripts can lead to reduced troubleshooting time and increased productivity.

PowerShell also allows for dynamic typing, meaning that variables can change types as needed during script execution. This feature is particularly useful in scenarios where data types may not be known in advance, such as when processing user input or retrieving information from external sources. However, while this flexibility can enhance productivity, it is essential to implement proper error handling and validation measures to ensure that scripts behave as expected. For IT professionals managing compliance and security, this attention to detail is critical in mitigating risks associated with data handling.

Ultimately, mastering variables and data types in PowerShell is not just about syntax; it encompasses a broader strategy for effective network management. By leveraging these tools, small businesses can automate routine tasks, enhance their operational efficiency, and better align their IT practices with business objectives. As network engineers and system administrators become proficient in using variables and data types, they will find themselves better equipped to tackle the challenges of modern IT environments, from cloud management to DevOps integration, ensuring compliance and security along the way.

©THE BOOK OF POWERSHELL
Copyrighted Material

ⒶISSO.TECH.ENTERPRISES

Control Structures and Flow Management

In the realm of PowerShell, control structures and flow management are essential concepts that enable IT professionals, system administrators, and network engineers to create efficient and effective scripts. These constructs facilitate decision-making processes, enabling scripts to respond dynamically to varying conditions and parameters. Understanding how to employ control structures such as loops, conditionals, and error handling is crucial for automating tasks and managing network resources seamlessly. This knowledge not only enhances productivity but also ensures that scripts can handle real-world complexities encountered in small business environments.

At the core of flow management in PowerShell are conditional statements, primarily the `if`, `else`, and `switch` constructs. These tools allow users to execute specific blocks of code based on the evaluation of conditions. For instance, in network management, you might use an `if` statement to check the status of a server before executing a command to restart it. By leveraging these control structures, administrators can build scripts that make intelligent decisions, reducing the likelihood of errors and improving the overall reliability of automated tasks. The `switch` statement can be particularly beneficial when dealing with multiple conditions, providing a cleaner and more organized approach than nested `if` statements.

Loops, another critical aspect of control structures, enable repetitive execution of code blocks. PowerShell offers several

Copyrighted Material
VICTOR P HENDERSON | ISSO-TECH ENTERPRISES™

CERTIFIED ETHICAL HACKER C|EH
ISSO-TECH PRESS™

types of loops, including `for`, `foreach`, and `while` loops, each serving different purposes. For example, a `foreach` loop can be used to iterate over a collection of network devices, applying specific commands to each device in a systematic manner. This capability is invaluable for tasks such as bulk configuration changes or monitoring the status of multiple servers. By integrating loops into scripts, IT professionals can significantly reduce the time and effort required to manage network resources, thereby enhancing operational efficiency.

Error handling is an often-overlooked element of flow management that is vital for creating robust PowerShell scripts. The use of `try`, `catch`, and `finally` blocks allows users to anticipate potential issues and respond appropriately. For instance, when managing cloud resources in Azure or AWS, the ability to gracefully handle exceptions can prevent cascading failures and ensure that critical operations continue to run smoothly. Implementing effective error handling not only improves script resilience but also aids in compliance and security by ensuring that scripts do not leave systems in an inconsistent state after encountering problems.

In conclusion, mastering control structures and flow management in PowerShell is essential for small businesses aiming to streamline their IT operations. By employing conditionals and loops, system administrators can create scripts that respond intelligently to various scenarios, while effective error handling ensures reliability and compliance. As small businesses increasingly rely on automation for network management and other IT tasks, understanding these concepts will empower IT

©THE BOOK OF POWERSHELL
Copyrighted Material

@ISSO.TECH.ENTERPRISES

Copyrighted Material

professionals to harness the full potential of PowerShell, driving greater efficiency, security, and success in their operations.

Functions and Modules in PowerShell

Functions and modules in PowerShell are pivotal tools for enhancing productivity and efficiency in network management, particularly for small businesses. As organizations strive to automate routine tasks and streamline their operations, understanding how to create and utilize functions and modules becomes essential. Functions allow users to encapsulate code into reusable blocks, while modules provide a way to package these functions and related resources, promoting better organization and sharing of scripts across teams or departments.

Creating functions in PowerShell is a straightforward yet powerful way to enhance script functionality. A function can be defined to perform a specific task, such as retrieving network configurations or managing user accounts. By using parameters, functions can be made flexible and adaptable to different scenarios, allowing IT professionals to tailor their scripts to meet varying business needs. Small businesses benefit from this capability as it reduces redundancy and minimizes the potential for errors, thereby increasing overall operational efficiency.

Modules take the concept of functions a step further by grouping related functions, variables, and other resources into a single unit. This modularization is particularly beneficial in environments where multiple scripts are in use. It enables system administrators

Copyrighted Material
VICTOR P HENDERSON | ISSO-TECH ENTERPRISES™

CERTIFIED ETHICAL HACKER C|EH
ISSO-TECH PRESS™

and network engineers to maintain a clean and organized codebase, making it easier to manage and update scripts as business requirements evolve. For small businesses looking to implement best practices in PowerShell, leveraging modules not only simplifies code management but also facilitates collaboration among IT staff.

In addition to enhancing organization, modules support the principles of code reuse and sharing. PowerShell allows users to import modules from various sources, including those created internally or from reputable community repositories. This capability is particularly advantageous for organizations that leverage cloud services, such as Azure or AWS, as it enables the integration of pre-built solutions tailored for cloud management. Furthermore, adopting modules can significantly improve security and compliance efforts, as they can be designed to include only the necessary functions, reducing the attack surface and ensuring that sensitive operations are encapsulated within controlled boundaries.

As businesses continue to embrace automation and DevOps practices, mastering functions and modules in PowerShell will be crucial. By developing a solid understanding of these concepts, IT professionals can effectively streamline their workflows, enhance security posture, and ensure that their network management strategies align with broader organizational goals. For small businesses, investing time in learning and implementing PowerShell functions and modules can lead to substantial long-term benefits, including reduced operational costs, improved service delivery, and greater agility in responding to changing market demands.

©THE BOOK OF POWERSHELL
Copyrighted Material

④ISSO.TECH.ENTERPRISES

©THE BOOK OF POWERSHELL

Copyrighted Material

POWERSHELL

Copyrighted Material

VICTOR P HENDERSON | ISSO-TECH ENTERPRISES™

CERTIFIED ETHICAL HACKER C|EH

ISSO-TECH PRESS™

VICTOR P HENDERSON | ISSO-TECH ENTERPRISES™

CERTIFIED ETHICAL HACKER C|EH
Copyrighted Material

CHAPTER 4
AUTOMATING
NETWORK TASKS

©THE BOOK OF POWERSHELL
Copyrighted Material

@ISSO.TECH.ENTERPRISES

Copyrighted Material

CHAPTER 4 | POWERSHELL AUTOMATION
SCRIPTING NETWORK TASK

Scripting Basics for Automation

Scripting is a powerful tool for automating routine tasks in network management, making it an essential skill for small businesses, IT professionals, system administrators, and network engineers. PowerShell, as a versatile scripting language, allows users to streamline operations, enhance productivity, and reduce the likelihood of human error in system management. Understanding the foundational elements of PowerShell scripting is crucial for effectively leveraging its capabilities in various IT environments, including cloud management, security compliance, and database administration.

The first step in mastering PowerShell scripting is familiarizing oneself with the basic syntax and structure that PowerShell employs. Scripts in PowerShell are composed of commands known as cmdlets, which perform specific functions. Each cmdlet follows a verb-noun format, such as "Get-Process" or "Set-Item," making it intuitive for users to understand their purpose. Additionally, PowerShell supports the use of variables, loops, and conditionals, allowing for more complex and dynamic scripts. Small businesses can benefit by automating repetitive tasks such as user account creation, system updates, and resource monitoring, freeing up valuable time for IT staff to focus on more strategic initiatives.

Copyrighted Material
VICTOR P HENDERSON | ISSO-TECH ENTERPRISES™

CERTIFIED ETHICAL HACKER C|EH
ISSO-TECH PRESS™

229.320.151.8

Error handling is another critical aspect of scripting that should not be overlooked. In any automated process, the potential for errors exists, and it is essential to incorporate error-handling mechanisms within your scripts. PowerShell provides several built-in features to manage errors effectively, such as try-catch-finally blocks, which allow users to capture and respond to exceptions gracefully. By implementing robust error handling, small businesses can ensure that their automated processes run smoothly, minimizing downtime and maintaining system integrity.

Moreover, small businesses should take advantage of PowerShell's ability to interact with various systems and applications, which is particularly beneficial in cloud environments like Azure and AWS. By utilizing the Azure and AWS modules available in PowerShell, administrators can automate tasks such as resource provisioning, configuration management, and cost monitoring. This integration not only simplifies operations but also enhances compliance and security measures by ensuring that best practices are consistently followed across all platforms.

Lastly, documentation and version control are essential practices that contribute to the long-term success of PowerShell scripting efforts. As scripts evolve, maintaining clear documentation and version history allows teams to track changes, identify issues, and collaborate effectively. Utilizing tools such as Git for version control can enhance teamwork and ensure that scripts remain secure and functional over time. By prioritizing documentation and version control, small businesses can foster a culture of continuous improvement in their scripting practices, ultimately leading to more efficient network management and better alignment with business objectives.

©**THE BOOK OF POWERSHELL**
Copyrighted Material

@ISSO.TECH.ENTERPRISES

Scheduling Tasks with PowerShell

In the realm of network management for small businesses, efficient task scheduling is paramount. PowerShell offers a robust framework for automating routine tasks, enabling IT professionals, system administrators, and network engineers to streamline operations and enhance productivity. By leveraging the capabilities of PowerShell, users can create scripts that not only automate processes but also ensure that these tasks are executed at optimal times, thereby reducing manual intervention and minimizing the risk of human error.

To get started with task scheduling in PowerShell, it's essential to understand the use of the Task Scheduler. This built-in Windows feature allows users to run scripts and programs at predefined intervals or in response to specific events. PowerShell provides cmdlets such as `New-ScheduledTask`, `Register-ScheduledTask`, and `Set-ScheduledTask`, which facilitate the creation and management of scheduled tasks. By utilizing these cmdlets, system administrators can efficiently schedule maintenance scripts, backup routines, and other critical tasks, ensuring that essential operations occur seamlessly without constant oversight.

When automating tasks with PowerShell, best practices should be observed to enhance reliability and security. For instance, it is advisable to execute scripts with the least privilege necessary to perform their function, thereby limiting potential security risks. Additionally, incorporating logging mechanisms within scripts can provide valuable insights into task execution, helping teams

Copyrighted Material
VICTOR P HENDERSON | ISSO-TECH ENTERPRISES™

CERTIFIED ETHICAL HACKER C|EH
ISSO-TECH PRESS™

229.320.151.8

troubleshoot issues and maintain compliance with organizational policies. By adhering to these best practices, small businesses can ensure that their automated tasks not only save time but also operate within the confines of security and compliance requirements.

Integrating PowerShell with cloud management platforms, such as Azure and AWS, can further expand the capabilities of task scheduling. Cloud environments often require dynamic resource management, and PowerShell is equipped with modules that allow for the automation of cloud-related tasks. For example, administrators can schedule scripts that manage virtual machines, monitor resource usage, and optimize costs based on predefined criteria. This integration not only enhances operational efficiency but also ensures that cloud resources are utilized effectively, contributing to the overall success of small business IT strategies.

In conclusion, mastering task scheduling with PowerShell is an invaluable skill for small businesses aiming to optimize their IT operations. By effectively utilizing the Task Scheduler and adhering to best practices, IT professionals can automate critical tasks, enhance security, and integrate with cloud management solutions. This approach not only improves workflow efficiency but also enables organizations to focus on strategic initiatives rather than getting bogged down by routine maintenance tasks. As small businesses continue to embrace technology, leveraging PowerShell for task scheduling will be a key component in driving operational success.

Copyrighted Material

Examples of Automated Network Management Tasks

Automated network management tasks are crucial for small businesses aiming to optimize their IT operations while minimizing manual intervention. By leveraging PowerShell, IT professionals can streamline various network management functions, ensuring efficiency and reliability. This subchapter explores several practical examples of automated network management tasks that can be implemented using PowerShell scripting, catering specifically to the needs of small businesses.

One common task that can be automated is the monitoring of device statuses across the network. Using PowerShell scripts, administrators can regularly check the health of network devices such as switches, routers, and firewalls. By utilizing cmdlets like `Get-NetAdapter` and `Test-Connection`, scripts can be written to ping devices and log their response times. This automation not only saves time but also helps in promptly identifying and resolving connectivity issues, ensuring that the network remains operational.

Another significant area for automation is user account management. Small businesses often face challenges in managing user permissions and access levels, especially as they grow. PowerShell can facilitate the automation of user account creation, modification, and deletion using cmdlets such as `New-ADUser`, `Set-ADUser`, and `Remove-ADUser`. By implementing scripts that integrate with Active Directory, IT administrators can ensure

Copyrighted Material
VICTOR P HENDERSON | ISSO-TECH ENTERPRISES™

CERTIFIED ETHICAL HACKER C|EH
ISSO-TECH PRESS™

that only authorized personnel have access to critical systems, thereby enhancing security and compliance.

Network configuration management is also a prime candidate for automation. PowerShell's ability to interact with various network devices allows for the automation of configuration changes, such as updating firewall rules or modifying VLAN settings. Scripts can be designed to pull current configurations using `Get-Content` and apply changes in a systematic manner. This not only reduces the risk of human error but also ensures that changes are documented and can be easily rolled back if necessary.

In addition to monitoring and configuration tasks, automated reporting is a vital aspect of network management. PowerShell can generate detailed reports on network performance metrics, user activity, and system health. By scheduling scripts with the Task Scheduler, administrators can produce regular reports that provide insights into network usage and potential bottlenecks. This data can inform strategic decisions, allowing small businesses to allocate resources more effectively and improve overall network performance.

Finally, integrating PowerShell with cloud management platforms such as Azure and AWS can further enhance network management capabilities. Automating tasks such as provisioning cloud resources, configuring virtual networks, and managing security groups can significantly reduce the operational overhead for small businesses. By utilizing PowerShell modules specific to these cloud services, IT professionals can create scripts that unify on-premises and cloud-based network management, fostering a more cohesive IT environment. This level of automation not only

Copyrighted Material

enhances efficiency but also positions small businesses to leverage cloud technologies effectively, ensuring they remain competitive in an increasingly digital landscape.

Copyrighted Material
VICTOR P HENDERSON | ISSO-TECH ENTERPRISES™

CERTIFIED ETHICAL HACKER C|EH
ISSO-TECH PRESS™

VICTOR P HENDERSON | ISSO-TECH ENTERPRISES™

CERTIFIED ETHICAL HACKER C|EH
Copyrighted Material

THIS PAGE LEFT BLANK INTENTIONALLY!

©THE BOOK OF POWERSHELL
Copyrighted Material

@ISSO.TECH.ENTERPRISES

©**THE BOOK OF POWERSHELL**

Copyrighted Material

POWERSHELL

Copyrighted Material

VICTOR P HENDERSON | ISSO-TECH ENTERPRISES™

CERTIFIED ETHICAL HACKER C|EH

ISSO-TECH PRESS™

229.320.151.8

VICTOR P HENDERSON | ISSO-TECH ENTERPRISES™

CERTIFIED ETHICAL HACKER C|EH
Copyrighted Material

CHAPTER 5
POWERSHELL
NETWORK
CONFIGURATION

©THE BOOK OF POWERSHELL
Copyrighted Material

@ISSO.TECH.ENTERPRISES

Copyrighted Material

CHAPTER 5 | POWERSHELL
NETWORK CONFIGURATION

Managing Network Interfaces

Managing network interfaces is a critical component of network administration that directly impacts performance, security, and reliability. In a small business environment, where resources may be limited, understanding how to efficiently manage network interfaces using PowerShell can lead to significant improvements in operational efficiency. This subchapter aims to equip IT professionals, system administrators, and network engineers with the necessary skills to leverage PowerShell for effective network interface management.

PowerShell provides a robust framework for managing network interfaces through a comprehensive set of cmdlets that allow administrators to configure, monitor, and troubleshoot network settings. Using cmdlets like Get-NetAdapter, Set-NetAdapter, and Remove-NetAdapter, administrators can easily retrieve information about network adapters, modify their properties, and remove unused interfaces. The simplicity and power of these commands enable small businesses to optimize their networking hardware, ensuring that resources are utilized effectively without the need for extensive manual intervention.

Automation is another cornerstone of PowerShell's utility in managing network interfaces. By creating scripts that automate

Copyrighted Material
VICTOR P HENDERSON | ISSO-TECH ENTERPRISES™

CERTIFIED ETHICAL HACKER C|EH
ISSO-TECH PRESS™

routine tasks such as updating adapter settings or monitoring interface statuses, system administrators can significantly reduce the risk of human error and free up valuable time for other critical IT initiatives. For example, a scheduled script could check the status of all network interfaces every hour and send alerts if any interfaces become disconnected. This not only enhances operational oversight but also allows for proactive measures in network management.

Security is an ever-increasing concern for small businesses, and managing network interfaces plays a crucial role in maintaining a secure environment. PowerShell enables administrators to configure advanced security settings for network interfaces, including the implementation of VLANs and the enforcement of firewall rules. Additionally, PowerShell can be used to audit network interface settings, ensuring compliance with organizational policies and industry standards. By regularly reviewing and adjusting these settings through automated scripts, businesses can mitigate vulnerabilities and protect sensitive data more effectively.

Finally, integration with cloud management platforms such as Azure and AWS further enriches the capabilities of PowerShell in managing network interfaces. With the rise of hybrid cloud architectures, small businesses can benefit from using PowerShell to manage both on-premises and cloud-based network interfaces seamlessly. This chapter will also address best practices for integrating PowerShell scripts with cloud services, helping businesses streamline their network management processes. By mastering these techniques, IT professionals can ensure that their

Copyrighted Material

network infrastructure is not only well-maintained but also aligned with the dynamic needs of the business.

Copyrighted Material
VICTOR P HENDERSON | ISSO-TECH ENTERPRISES™

CERTIFIED ETHICAL HACKER C|EH
ISSO-TECH PRESS™

Configuring IP Addresses and DNS

Configuring IP addresses and DNS settings is a fundamental aspect of network management that directly impacts the performance and reliability of a small business's IT infrastructure. In the context of PowerShell, these tasks can be automated and managed efficiently, allowing IT professionals, system administrators, and network engineers to focus on strategic initiatives rather than repetitive configuration tasks. This subchapter will delve into the essential commands and scripts for configuring IP addresses and DNS, providing practical examples to enhance your network management capabilities.

PowerShell offers a robust set of cmdlets specifically designed for network configuration. The `Get-NetIPAddress`, `New-NetIPAddress`, and `Remove-NetIPAddress` cmdlets are invaluable for managing IP addresses dynamically. For instance, when deploying new devices or reconfiguring existing ones, administrators can utilize these cmdlets to assign static or dynamic IP addresses, ensuring seamless connectivity within the organization. Understanding how to leverage these commands effectively can save time and reduce the potential for human error during manual configurations.

In addition to IP address management, configuring DNS settings is critical for ensuring that network resources are easily accessible. The `Add-DnsServerResourceRecordA` and `Remove-DnsServerResourceRecordA` cmdlets allow administrators to manage A records, which map hostnames to IP addresses. This capability is essential for small businesses that rely on internal and external domain names for various applications, such as email

©THE BOOK OF POWERSHELL
Copyrighted Material

servers and web hosting. Automating these configurations not only streamlines the process but also enhances the accuracy of DNS records, minimizing downtime and connectivity issues.

Security considerations are paramount when configuring IP addresses and DNS settings. PowerShell provides the ability to enforce security policies through the `Set-NetIPInterface` cmdlet, which allows administrators to configure settings such as DHCP, IP filtering, and more. Additionally, utilizing the `Get-DnsServerZone` cmdlet can help ensure that DNS zones are properly secured and maintained. By integrating security best practices into the IP and DNS configuration processes, small businesses can protect their networks from unauthorized access and potential cyber threats.

To illustrate the power of PowerShell in network management, consider a scenario where a small business is migrating its infrastructure to a cloud platform like Azure. The `Set-AzVirtualNetworkSubnetConfig` cmdlet can be utilized to configure subnets within the Azure environment, while also allowing for the integration of on-premises DNS servers. This example highlights the versatility of PowerShell, enabling IT professionals to manage complex network configurations across diverse environments efficiently. By mastering these techniques, small businesses can achieve greater operational efficiency and resilience in their network management strategies.

Copyrighted Material
VICTOR P HENDERSON | ISSO-TECH ENTERPRISES™

CERTIFIED ETHICAL HACKER C|EH
ISSO-TECH PRESS™

Monitoring Network Performance

Monitoring network performance is a critical aspect of maintaining a robust IT infrastructure, especially for small businesses where resources may be limited. In this subchapter, we will explore how PowerShell can be effectively utilized to monitor network performance, providing IT professionals, system administrators, and network engineers with the tools necessary to ensure optimal network functionality. By leveraging PowerShell's capabilities for automation and integration, businesses can proactively identify issues, analyze performance metrics, and enhance overall network reliability.

One of the primary advantages of using PowerShell for network performance monitoring is its ability to collect and analyze data in real time. PowerShell scripts can be designed to query network devices, gather performance metrics such as bandwidth usage, latency, and packet loss, and present this data in a comprehensive format. This enables IT professionals to not only monitor the current state of the network but also to track historical performance trends. By automating the data collection process, small businesses can save valuable time while ensuring that critical metrics are consistently monitored.

In addition to real-time monitoring, PowerShell can be employed to set up alerts and notifications for specific performance thresholds. For example, if bandwidth usage exceeds a predefined limit or if latency spikes beyond acceptable levels, a PowerShell script can trigger alerts to notify the relevant personnel. This proactive approach allows system administrators to address issues before they escalate into significant problems, ultimately minimizing downtime and enhancing productivity. PowerShell's integration with various notification systems, such as email or messaging platforms, further facilitates timely communication and incident response.

Another significant aspect of network performance monitoring is the ability to generate reports for analysis and compliance purposes. PowerShell can be utilized to automate the generation of detailed performance reports, summarizing key metrics and trends over specified periods. These reports can be invaluable for small businesses in assessing their network's health, justifying upgrades, or demonstrating compliance with industry standards. Furthermore, the flexibility of PowerShell allows these reports to be customized according to the specific needs of the business, ensuring relevance and utility.

Lastly, the integration of PowerShell with cloud management platforms like Azure and AWS enhances monitoring capabilities for hybrid and cloud-based environments. As more small businesses migrate to these platforms, understanding how to monitor network performance effectively within these ecosystems becomes paramount. PowerShell provides cmdlets that can interact directly with cloud services, enabling users to track network performance across both on-premises and cloud resources. This holistic view is essential for optimizing network performance and ensuring seamless operations, particularly in the increasingly interconnected digital landscape that small businesses navigate today.

Copyrighted Material
VICTOR P HENDERSON | ISSO-TECH ENTERPRISES™

CERTIFIED ETHICAL HACKER C|EH
ISSO-TECH PRESS™

VICTOR P HENDERSON | ISSO-TECH ENTERPRISES™

CERTIFIED ETHICAL HACKER C|EH
Copyrighted Material

THIS PAGE LEFT BLANK INTENTIONALLY!

©THE BOOK OF POWERSHELL
Copyrighted Material

@ISSO.TECH.ENTERPRISES

©THE BOOK OF POWERSHELL

Copyrighted Material

POWERSHELL

Copyrighted Material

VICTOR P HENDERSON | ISSO-TECH ENTERPRISES™

CERTIFIED ETHICAL HACKER C|EH

ISSO-TECH PRESS™

VICTOR P HENDERSON | ISSO-TECH ENTERPRISES™

CERTIFIED ETHICAL HACKER C|EH
Copyrighted Material

CHAPTER 6: POWERSHELL FOR NETWORK SECURITY

©THE BOOK OF POWERSHELL
Copyrighted Material

@ISSO.TECH.ENTERPRISES

Copyrighted Material

CHAPTER 6 | POWERSHELL FOR SECURITY
NETWORK SECURITY

Implementing Security Policies

Implementing effective security policies is crucial for small businesses looking to protect their digital assets and ensure compliance with industry standards. In the landscape of rapidly advancing technology, small businesses often face unique challenges in managing their network security. PowerShell emerges as a powerful tool that not only automates routine tasks but also provides a robust framework for implementing and managing security policies. By leveraging PowerShell's capabilities, IT professionals, system administrators, and network engineers can create tailored security solutions that align with their organizational needs.

The first step in implementing security policies using PowerShell involves assessing the current security posture of the network. Conducting a comprehensive security audit allows organizations to identify vulnerabilities and potential areas of risk. PowerShell scripts can be employed to gather data on system configurations, user permissions, and installed software, providing a clear picture of the existing security landscape. By analyzing this data, IT professionals can develop informed policies that enhance security while accommodating the specific requirements of their business operations.

Copyrighted Material
VICTOR P HENDERSON | ISSO-TECH ENTERPRISES™

CERTIFIED ETHICAL HACKER C|EH
ISSO-TECH PRESS™

229.320.151.8

Once vulnerabilities are identified, the next phase is the creation of security policies that address these concerns. PowerShell enables the automation of policy enforcement, ensuring that security measures are consistently applied across the network. For example, scripts can be used to manage user access controls, enforce password policies, and configure firewall settings. By automating these processes, small businesses can reduce human error and enhance compliance with regulatory requirements. Additionally, PowerShell's integration with cloud platforms like Azure and AWS allows for seamless management of security policies in cloud environments, further strengthening the overall security framework.

Monitoring and maintaining security policies is an ongoing process that requires regular review and updates. PowerShell provides tools for continuous monitoring through scripting and automation, allowing IT professionals to track compliance and detect anomalies in real time. By setting up automated reporting and alert systems, organizations can quickly respond to potential security breaches or policy violations. This proactive approach not only mitigates risks but also fosters a culture of security awareness within the organization, ensuring that all employees understand the importance of adhering to established policies.

In conclusion, implementing security policies through PowerShell is a strategic approach that empowers small businesses to enhance their network security. By utilizing the automation capabilities of PowerShell, IT professionals can streamline the assessment, creation, enforcement, and monitoring of security policies. This not only improves the efficiency of security management but also aligns with best practices in compliance and risk management. As

©THE BOOK OF POWERSHELL
Copyrighted Material

@ISSO.TECH.ENTERPRISES

Copyrighted Material

small businesses continue to navigate the complexities of the digital landscape, effective security policies will remain a cornerstone of sustainable success.

Copyrighted Material
VICTOR P HENDERSON | ISSO-TECH ENTERPRISES™

CERTIFIED ETHICAL HACKER C|EH
ISSO-TECH PRESS™

Auditing and Compliance with PowerShell

In the contemporary landscape of network management, auditing and compliance are critical components for small businesses aiming to secure their IT environments. PowerShell, with its robust scripting capabilities and extensive command set, offers IT professionals, system administrators, and network engineers powerful tools to establish and maintain compliance with various regulatory frameworks. This subchapter explores how PowerShell can be leveraged for effective auditing practices, ensuring that organizations not only meet compliance requirements but also enhance their overall security posture.

Auditing involves the systematic examination of an organization's IT systems and processes to ensure that they are operating effectively and in accordance with established policies and regulations. PowerShell facilitates this process by providing cmdlets that can generate detailed reports on system configurations, user access, and changes made within the environment. For instance, using commands to query Active Directory can yield insights into user permissions and group memberships, thereby identifying potential security risks. By automating these auditing tasks through PowerShell scripts, small businesses can save time and resources while maintaining a continuous compliance stance.

Compliance requirements can vary significantly depending on the industry and specific regulations governing data security, privacy, and operational integrity. PowerShell supports compliance efforts by enabling the automation of compliance checks and the generation of documentation required for audits. For example,

©**THE BOOK OF POWERSHELL**
Copyrighted Material

@ISSO.TECH.ENTERPRISES

Copyrighted Material

scripts can be created to verify that security settings align with standards such as NIST, HIPAA, or GDPR. These scripts can run on a scheduled basis, providing regular reports that highlight compliance status and any deviations from established norms, thereby allowing organizations to proactively address issues before they escalate.

In addition to generating reports, PowerShell can facilitate compliance through real-time monitoring and alerting. By implementing logging and monitoring scripts, small businesses can track significant changes to their systems and configurations. PowerShell's ability to integrate with other systems, such as SIEM (Security Information and Event Management) tools, enhances its effectiveness in providing immediate feedback on compliance-related events. For instance, an automated script can be set up to notify administrators when unauthorized changes to critical configurations are detected, ensuring that any deviations are swiftly addressed.

Furthermore, the role of PowerShell in compliance extends to training and documentation. Small businesses often face challenges in ensuring that their staff is aware of compliance requirements and best practices. PowerShell can be utilized to create educational scripts that not only demonstrate compliance procedures but also serve as a reference for system administrators and IT professionals. By embedding compliance knowledge within PowerShell scripts, organizations can foster a culture of awareness and accountability, ultimately contributing to a more secure and compliant IT environment. In summary, auditing and compliance through PowerShell not only streamline processes but also empower small

Copyrighted Material

VICTOR P HENDERSON | ISSO-TECH ENTERPRISES™

CERTIFIED ETHICAL HACKER C|EH
ISSO-TECH PRESS™

VICTOR P HENDERSON | ISSO-TECH ENTERPRISES™

CERTIFIED ETHICAL HACKER C|EH
Copyrighted Material

businesses to navigate the complexities of regulatory requirements with confidence.

©THE BOOK OF POWERSHELL
Copyrighted Material

@ISSO.TECH.ENTERPRISES

Copyrighted Material

Securing PowerShell Scripts

Securing PowerShell scripts is a critical aspect of managing network systems, especially for small businesses that may not have extensive IT resources. As PowerShell becomes increasingly integral to automation and cloud management, it is vital to recognize the security implications that come with scripting. Small businesses often face unique challenges, such as limited budgets and staff, making it essential to adopt best practices that not only enhance operational efficiency but also safeguard sensitive information against potential threats.

One fundamental strategy for securing PowerShell scripts involves implementing proper access controls. Administrators should ensure that scripts are stored in secure locations with restricted access permissions. By using file system permissions and Active Directory groups, only authorized users should be allowed to modify or execute the scripts. Additionally, leveraging role-based access control (RBAC) can help ensure that users have the minimum level of permissions necessary to perform their tasks, thus reducing the risk of accidental or malicious changes.

Another crucial aspect of securing PowerShell scripts is the use of code signing. Code signing involves digitally signing scripts with a trusted certificate, which verifies the authenticity and integrity of the script. This practice is particularly important for businesses that rely on scripts to execute critical operations or handle sensitive data. By enforcing execution policies that only allow signed scripts to run, organizations can significantly reduce the risk of running

Copyrighted Material
VICTOR P HENDERSON | ISSO-TECH ENTERPRISES™

CERTIFIED ETHICAL HACKER C|EH
ISSO-TECH PRESS™

potentially harmful or unauthorized code. This is a vital step in maintaining compliance with security policies and regulatory requirements.

In addition to access controls and code signing, incorporating logging and monitoring practices can enhance the security of PowerShell scripts. Implementing comprehensive logging allows administrators to track script executions, identify anomalies, and respond promptly to any suspicious activities. PowerShell's built-in logging capabilities, combined with centralized logging solutions, enable businesses to maintain an audit trail that can be invaluable for compliance and incident response. Regularly reviewing logs can help detect unauthorized access attempts or malicious modifications, thus providing an additional layer of security.

Finally, small businesses should establish a robust training program for their IT staff regarding PowerShell security best practices. As technology evolves, so do the threats associated with it. Regular training sessions can help ensure that IT professionals are up to date with the latest security features and practices related to PowerShell. This includes understanding how to write secure scripts, recognize potential vulnerabilities, and implement security measures effectively. By fostering a culture of security awareness, small businesses can empower their teams to proactively protect their network infrastructure from emerging threats.

©THE BOOK OF POWERSHELL
Copyrighted Material

@ISSO.TECH.ENTERPRISES

©THE BOOK OF POWERSHELL

Copyrighted Material

POWERSHELL

Copyrighted Material

VICTOR P HENDERSON | ISSO-TECH ENTERPRISES™

CERTIFIED ETHICAL HACKER C|EH

ISSO-TECH PRESS™

VICTOR P HENDERSON | ISSO-TECH ENTERPRISES™

CERTIFIED ETHICAL HACKER C|EH
Copyrighted Material

CHAPTER 7: TROUBLESHOOTING NETWORKS WITH POWERSHELL

©THE BOOK OF POWERSHELL
Copyrighted Material

@ISSO.TECH.ENTERPRISES

Copyrighted Material

CHAPTER 7 | POWERSHELL DIAGNOSTICS
NETWORK TROUBLESHOOTING

Common Network Problems and Solutions

In today's interconnected business environment, small businesses often face a myriad of network problems that can disrupt operations and hinder productivity. Understanding these common issues and their resolutions is essential for IT professionals, system administrators, and network engineers who are tasked with maintaining robust and efficient network systems. This subchapter will delve into prevalent network challenges, focusing on how PowerShell can be effectively utilized to diagnose and rectify these issues, thereby ensuring seamless network management.

One of the most frequent network problems encountered by small businesses is connectivity issues. These can stem from a variety of sources, including faulty hardware, misconfigured settings, or ISP-related disruptions. When connectivity problems arise, the first step is to assess the state of the network interfaces and connections. PowerShell offers a suite of cmdlets such as Get-NetAdapter and Test-NetConnection, which allow administrators to examine the status of network adapters and perform connectivity tests to identify the source of the issue. By leveraging these tools, IT professionals can quickly pinpoint whether the problem lies within the local network or if it is an external factor, allowing for a more focused troubleshooting approach.

Copyrighted Material
VICTOR P HENDERSON | ISSO-TECH ENTERPRISES™

CERTIFIED ETHICAL HACKER C|EH
ISSO-TECH PRESS™

Another common issue is network performance degradation, often manifested through slow data transfer rates or latency spikes. These performance issues can be attributed to various factors, including bandwidth congestion, network configuration errors, or even external interference. PowerShell can assist in diagnosing these problems by enabling users to monitor network traffic and analyze performance metrics. Cmdlets like Get-NetTCPConnection and Get-NetIPStatistics can provide valuable insights into current connections and data transfer rates, helping administrators identify bottlenecks. Once identified, appropriate actions can be taken, such as optimizing router configurations or reallocating bandwidth to critical applications.

Security vulnerabilities present a significant challenge for small businesses, particularly as cyber threats continue to evolve. Network security issues can arise from outdated software, misconfigured firewall settings, or unauthorized access attempts. PowerShell provides an effective means of enhancing security posture through its scripting capabilities. Administrators can utilize scripts to automate regular security audits, check for open ports using Get-NetFirewallRule, and implement compliance checks against organizational policies. By proactively managing security through PowerShell, businesses can mitigate risks and respond swiftly to potential threats before they escalate.

Lastly, network configuration errors can lead to significant operational disruptions, especially in environments that rely on precise settings for their network infrastructure. These errors may include incorrect IP address assignments, subnet mask misconfigurations, or DNS issues. PowerShell simplifies the process of auditing and correcting network configurations. With

©THE BOOK OF POWERSHELL
Copyrighted Material

@ISSO.TECH.ENTERPRISES

Copyrighted Material

cmdlets like Get-DnsClient and Set-NetIPAddress, administrators can efficiently review and modify network settings. Furthermore, PowerShell scripts can be employed to enforce consistent configuration across multiple devices, reducing the likelihood of human error and ensuring compliance with best practices.

In conclusion, the ability to swiftly identify and resolve common network problems is critical for the success of small businesses. By harnessing the power of PowerShell, IT professionals and network engineers can effectively manage and troubleshoot their network environments. This not only minimizes downtime but also enhances overall productivity. As network challenges continue to evolve, mastering PowerShell will remain an invaluable skill for those dedicated to maintaining the integrity and efficiency of their business networks.

Copyrighted Material
VICTOR P HENDERSON | ISSO-TECH ENTERPRISES™

CERTIFIED ETHICAL HACKER C|EH
ISSO-TECH PRESS™

VICTOR P HENDERSON | ISSO-TECH ENTERPRISES™

CERTIFIED ETHICAL HACKER C|EH
Copyrighted Material

Using Cmdlets for Diagnostics

Using Cmdlets for Diagnostics

In the realm of network management, effective diagnostics are paramount for maintaining system integrity and optimizing performance. PowerShell, with its extensive library of cmdlets, provides invaluable tools that allow IT professionals and system administrators to conduct thorough diagnostics of their network environments. Cmdlets, which are specialized .NET classes designed to perform specific functions, enable users to automate and streamline various aspects of network monitoring and troubleshooting. This chapter explores the essential cmdlets for diagnostics and highlights their capabilities in addressing common issues faced by small businesses.

One of the primary advantages of using PowerShell cmdlets is their ability to gather detailed information about network configurations and statuses. Cmdlets such as `Get-NetIPAddress`, `Get-NetAdapter`, and `Get-NetRoute` allow users to retrieve information about IP addresses, network adapters, and routing tables, respectively. This information is crucial for diagnosing connectivity issues and understanding the overall health of the network. By leveraging these cmdlets, IT professionals can quickly pinpoint misconfigurations or failures that may be impacting network performance, enabling faster resolution of issues.

In addition to gathering information, PowerShell cmdlets also facilitate troubleshooting through their capabilities to test connectivity and performance. Cmdlets like `Test-Connection` and `Test-NetConnection` are instrumental in validating network paths

©THE BOOK OF POWERSHELL
Copyrighted Material

@ISSO.TECH.ENTERPRISES

and diagnosing potential bottlenecks. For instance, `Test-Connection` can be used to perform ping tests against remote hosts, while `Test-NetConnection` offers more advanced options, including determining the availability of specific ports and protocols. By incorporating these cmdlets into routine diagnostic procedures, system administrators can proactively identify and address issues before they escalate into more significant problems.

PowerShell's integration with event logs further enhances its diagnostic capabilities. Cmdlets such as `Get-EventLog` and `Get-WinEvent` allow users to access and analyze events recorded in the system logs. This feature is particularly useful for identifying trends or recurring issues that may not be immediately apparent through standard monitoring practices. By filtering and sorting through event logs, network engineers can uncover the root causes of anomalies, leading to more effective long-term solutions. Furthermore, automating the retrieval and analysis of these logs can save significant time and resources, allowing teams to focus on strategic initiatives rather than reactive troubleshooting.

Lastly, the ability to script and automate repetitive diagnostic tasks using PowerShell provides small businesses with a significant edge in network management. By creating custom scripts that utilize cmdlets for diagnostics, IT professionals can standardize their diagnostic procedures, ensuring consistency and reliability in their approach. This automation not only increases efficiency but also reduces the likelihood of human error during critical troubleshooting scenarios. As small businesses strive to optimize their IT resources, mastering PowerShell scripting for diagnostics

Copyrighted Material
VICTOR P HENDERSON | ISSO-TECH ENTERPRISES™

CERTIFIED ETHICAL HACKER C|EH
ISSO-TECH PRESS™

becomes an essential skill, empowering teams to maintain robust and resilient network environments.

Creating Troubleshooting Scripts

Creating effective troubleshooting scripts is a vital skill for IT professionals, system administrators, and network engineers, especially within the context of small business operations. These scripts serve as automated tools that can efficiently diagnose and resolve common network issues, leading to reduced downtime and improved productivity. The ability to quickly identify problems and implement solutions is essential in maintaining a functional and reliable IT environment, making the mastery of PowerShell scripting particularly beneficial for those in small business settings.

To begin with, troubleshooting scripts should be designed with clarity and simplicity in mind. A well-structured script not only identifies issues but also provides clear feedback to the user. This can include logging essential information, such as error messages, system status, and any actions taken. Utilizing PowerShell's built-in cmdlets and functions, you can create scripts that gather diagnostic data from various sources, including network interfaces, event logs, and system performance metrics. This foundational step allows you to create a comprehensive picture of the network's health, which is invaluable when addressing problems.

Next, integrating conditional logic into your troubleshooting scripts enhances their effectiveness. By employing functions like `if`, `else`, and `switch`, you can create scripts that adapt their behavior based on the data they collect. For example, a script could check the status of a network service and, based on the result, either restart the service, notify an administrator, or log the event

Copyrighted Material
VICTOR P HENDERSON | ISSO-TECH ENTERPRISES™

CERTIFIED ETHICAL HACKER C|EH
ISSO-TECH PRESS™

for future analysis. This level of automation not only streamlines the troubleshooting process but also minimizes the potential for human error, which can be particularly detrimental in high-stakes situations.

Moreover, incorporating error handling is crucial for robust troubleshooting scripts. PowerShell provides several mechanisms for managing exceptions, including `try`, `catch`, and `finally` blocks. By anticipating potential failures and gracefully handling them, your scripts can continue to operate smoothly without crashing or providing misleading results. Logging errors and unexpected outcomes also allows for post-mortem analysis, enabling IT professionals to refine their scripts and processes over time, ultimately leading to more resilient network management strategies.

Finally, it is essential to test and refine your troubleshooting scripts regularly. Network environments are dynamic, and what works today may not be effective tomorrow due to changes in infrastructure, software updates, or evolving business needs. Regular testing ensures that your scripts remain relevant and functional. Additionally, seeking feedback from colleagues or other IT professionals can provide new insights and improve the overall quality of your scripts. By adopting a proactive approach to script development and maintenance, small businesses can ensure that their IT systems run smoothly, making the most of their resources and enhancing their competitive edge.

©THE BOOK OF POWERSHELL
Copyrighted Material

@ISSO.TECH.ENTERPRISES

©**THE BOOK OF POWERSHELL**

Copyrighted Material

POWERSHELL

Copyrighted Material

VICTOR P HENDERSON | ISSO-TECH ENTERPRISES™

CERTIFIED ETHICAL HACKER C|EH

ISSO-TECH PRESS™

229.320.151.8

VICTOR P HENDERSON | ISSO-TECH ENTERPRISES™

CERTIFIED ETHICAL HACKER C|EH
Copyrighted Material

CHAPTER 8
INTEGRATING POWERSHELL WITH CLOUD SERVICES

©THE BOOK OF POWERSHELL
Copyrighted Material

@ISSO.TECH.ENTERPRISES

CHAPTER 8 | POWERSHELL INTERGRATION
CLOUD SERVICES

Connecting to Azure and AWS

Connecting to cloud services like Azure and AWS is a critical skill for IT professionals, system administrators, and network engineers, especially in the context of small business operations. The flexibility and scalability offered by these platforms enable organizations to optimize their resources and manage their IT infrastructure more effectively. PowerShell serves as a powerful tool in this endeavor, allowing users to automate tasks, manage virtual environments, and streamline workflows. This subchapter outlines the essential steps to connect to Azure and AWS, highlighting the benefits and best practices for small businesses.

To establish a connection with Azure, the first step involves installing the Azure PowerShell module. This can be accomplished by using the command `Install-Module -Name Az -AllowClobber -Scope CurrentUser`. Once the module is installed, users can authenticate to their Azure account by executing the command `Connect-AzAccount`. This command opens a prompt for user credentials, securely handling the authentication process. For small businesses that may not have dedicated IT resources, this streamlined process allows for quick access to Azure's extensive cloud services, facilitating efficient management of resources.

Similarly, connecting to AWS through PowerShell requires the installation of the AWS Tools for PowerShell. By using the

Copyrighted Material
VICTOR P HENDERSON | ISSO-TECH ENTERPRISES™

CERTIFIED ETHICAL HACKER C|EH
ISSO-TECH PRESS™

command `Install-Module -Name AWSPowerShell`, users can gain access to AWS services directly from the PowerShell environment. Authentication to AWS can be achieved using the `Set-AWSCredential` cmdlet, which allows users to specify their access key and secret key. This capability is particularly beneficial for small businesses that rely on cloud-based services for their operational needs, as it simplifies the management of resources across different cloud platforms.

Automation is a key advantage of using PowerShell for cloud management. Once connected to Azure or AWS, users can leverage PowerShell scripts to automate routine tasks such as resource provisioning, configuration management, and monitoring. For instance, a system administrator can write scripts to automatically scale resources based on usage metrics, thereby optimizing costs and improving performance. This automation not only saves time but also reduces the likelihood of human error, making it an invaluable strategy for small businesses striving for efficiency.

Security and compliance are paramount when managing cloud environments. PowerShell provides robust capabilities for implementing security measures and ensuring compliance with industry standards. Users can employ PowerShell scripts to audit configurations, manage access controls, and monitor activities within their Azure and AWS environments. By integrating security best practices into their PowerShell workflows, small businesses can protect sensitive data and maintain compliance, thereby reducing risks associated with cloud operations. As the reliance on cloud computing continues to grow, mastering these PowerShell

Copyrighted Material

techniques becomes essential for successful network management in a small business context.

Copyrighted Material
VICTOR P HENDERSON | ISSO-TECH ENTERPRISES™

CERTIFIED ETHICAL HACKER C|EH
ISSO-TECH PRESS™

Managing Network Resources in the Cloud

Managing network resources in the cloud presents unique challenges and opportunities for small businesses. As organizations increasingly migrate their infrastructure to cloud environments such as Microsoft Azure and Amazon Web Services (AWS), understanding how to efficiently manage network resources becomes crucial. This subchapter will explore strategies and best practices for utilizing PowerShell to optimize cloud network management, ensuring that small businesses can maintain control, enhance security, and improve overall operational efficiency.

PowerShell provides a powerful automation framework that can significantly streamline the management of cloud resources. By leveraging cmdlets specifically designed for cloud services, IT professionals can automate routine tasks such as provisioning, monitoring, and configuring network resources. For instance, using Azure PowerShell modules allows system administrators to create and manage virtual networks, subnets, and network security groups with ease. This automation not only reduces the time spent on manual configurations but also minimizes the potential for human error, which is essential for maintaining network integrity.

In addition to provisioning and configuration, monitoring network performance and security is a vital aspect of cloud resource management. PowerShell scripts can be employed to regularly check the status of network components, analyze traffic patterns, and identify potential security threats. For example, integrating PowerShell with Azure Monitor can enable automatic alerts based on predefined thresholds, allowing IT teams to respond proactively to issues before they escalate. This level of oversight is particularly

©THE BOOK OF POWERSHELL
Copyrighted Material

@ISSO.TECH.ENTERPRISES

Copyrighted Material

important for small businesses that may lack the extensive resources to dedicate to a full-time network management team.

Security and compliance within cloud environments also necessitate a strategic approach. PowerShell offers robust features to help enforce security policies and ensure compliance with industry standards. By utilizing scripts to automate security audits and access controls, network engineers can maintain a secure environment while also adhering to regulations. Additionally, leveraging PowerShell to implement role-based access control (RBAC) can restrict permissions to sensitive network resources, further enhancing the security posture of the organization.

Finally, the integration of PowerShell with DevOps practices can foster a collaborative environment for network management. By adopting Infrastructure as Code (IaC) principles, small businesses can utilize PowerShell scripts to define and manage their network resources declaratively. This approach not only enhances consistency in configurations but also facilitates easier updates and rollbacks when necessary. As cloud environments evolve, embracing these advanced techniques will empower small businesses to manage their network resources effectively, ensuring that they remain agile and competitive in an increasingly digital landscape.

Copyrighted Material
VICTOR P HENDERSON | ISSO-TECH ENTERPRISES™

CERTIFIED ETHICAL HACKER C|EH
ISSO-TECH PRESS™

Best Practices for Cloud Network Management

Effective cloud network management is critical for small businesses seeking to leverage the full potential of cloud technologies. With the increasing reliance on cloud services, it is essential for IT professionals and system administrators to adopt best practices that ensure efficient, secure, and reliable network operations. This subchapter discusses key strategies for managing cloud networks using PowerShell, emphasizing automation, security, and compliance.

One of the foremost best practices is the automation of routine tasks through PowerShell scripting. By automating repetitive processes such as resource provisioning, monitoring, and updates, small businesses can reduce the risk of human error and increase operational efficiency. Leveraging PowerShell's cmdlets tailored for cloud environments, such as those available in Azure and AWS modules, allows administrators to create scripts that can quickly deploy, configure, and manage cloud resources. This not only saves time but also enables IT teams to focus their efforts on more strategic initiatives that drive business growth.

Security and compliance must be at the forefront of cloud network management. Small businesses are often targets for cyber threats, making it critical to implement strong security measures. PowerShell provides robust capabilities for managing security configurations and policies across cloud environments. Utilizing features like Azure Policy and AWS Identity and Access Management (IAM) through PowerShell scripts can help ensure that resources are compliant with industry standards and organizational policies. Regular audits and the automation of

Copyrighted Material

security checks can further enhance this aspect, allowing for proactive identification and remediation of vulnerabilities.

Another best practice involves continuous monitoring and performance optimization of cloud networks. Employing PowerShell to create monitoring scripts enables IT professionals to track key performance metrics, such as network latency and resource utilization. By integrating these scripts with alerting mechanisms, businesses can promptly respond to potential issues, thus minimizing downtime and maintaining service quality. Additionally, leveraging PowerShell's capabilities to analyze and visualize performance data can help identify trends and facilitate informed decision-making regarding resource allocation and scaling.

Collaboration and documentation are also essential components of effective cloud network management. PowerShell can be used to maintain comprehensive documentation of network configurations, scripts, and procedures, ensuring that knowledge is easily accessible to all team members. This documentation not only aids in onboarding new staff but also serves as a valuable resource during troubleshooting and audits. Furthermore, fostering collaboration among IT teams through shared PowerShell modules and scripts can enhance collective expertise and improve overall network management practices.

In conclusion, implementing best practices for cloud network management is vital for small businesses looking to optimize their operations and ensure security. By focusing on automation,

Copyrighted Material
VICTOR P HENDERSON | ISSO-TECH ENTERPRISES™

CERTIFIED ETHICAL HACKER C|EH
ISSO-TECH PRESS™

VICTOR P HENDERSON | ISSO-TECH ENTERPRISES™

CERTIFIED ETHICAL HACKER C|EH
Copyrighted Material

security, continuous monitoring, and effective collaboration, IT professionals and network engineers can leverage PowerShell to create a resilient and efficient cloud infrastructure. As cloud technologies evolve, staying abreast of these practices will empower teams to adapt and thrive in an increasingly digital landscape.

©THE BOOK OF POWERSHELL
Copyrighted Material

@ISSO.TECH.ENTERPRISES

Copyrighted Material

POWERSHELL

Copyrighted Material

VICTOR P HENDERSON | ISSO-TECH ENTERPRISES™

CERTIFIED ETHICAL HACKER C|EH
ISSO-TECH PRESS™

VICTOR P HENDERSON | ISSO-TECH ENTERPRISES™

CERTIFIED ETHICAL HACKER C|EH
Copyrighted Material

CHAPTER 9
POWERSHELL
DATABASE
MANAGEMENT

©THE BOOK OF POWERSHELL
Copyrighted Material

@ISSO.TECH.ENTERPRISES

Copyrighted Material

CHAPTER 9 | POWERSHELL DATA CONTROL
DATABASE MANAGEMENT

Connecting to Databases with PowerShell

Connecting to databases using PowerShell is an essential skill for small businesses, IT professionals, system administrators, and network engineers. With the growing reliance on data-driven decision-making, the ability to interact with databases efficiently can significantly enhance operational workflows. PowerShell provides a versatile framework that allows users to connect to various database systems, execute queries, and manage data seamlessly. This subchapter will explore the fundamental techniques for establishing these connections, focusing on SQL Server, Azure SQL Database, and other common database platforms.

To begin, establishing a connection to a SQL Server database can be achieved using the `Invoke-Sqlcmd` cmdlet, which is included with the SQL Server module. This cmdlet not only allows for executing T-SQL commands directly from the PowerShell environment but also facilitates the retrieval of data in a structured format. By leveraging this capability, system administrators can automate routine database tasks such as backups, updates, and data extraction. Additionally, it is crucial to manage authentication effectively, whether using Windows Authentication or SQL Server Authentication, to ensure secure access to sensitive data.

Copyrighted Material
VICTOR P HENDERSON | ISSO-TECH ENTERPRISES™

CERTIFIED ETHICAL HACKER C|EH
ISSO-TECH PRESS™

For small businesses utilizing cloud services, PowerShell offers robust capabilities for connecting to Azure SQL Database. The `SqlServer` module can be employed to manage interactions with the cloud database effectively. By using the `New-AzSqlDatabaseConnectionString` cmdlet, users can construct a connection string that incorporates necessary credentials and settings. This capability not only simplifies the management of database connections but also facilitates the automation of cloud-based data operations, allowing businesses to scale their database management practices in line with their growth.

In addition to SQL Server and Azure, PowerShell also supports connections to other database systems, such as MySQL and PostgreSQL, through the use of appropriate .NET data providers. By loading the relevant assembly, users can create and execute commands with these databases, thereby broadening the scope of data management operations. This versatility is particularly beneficial for organizations that utilize multiple database systems, enabling them to maintain a unified approach to data handling across platforms.

Lastly, ensuring security and compliance while connecting to databases is paramount for any small business. PowerShell provides several methods to secure sensitive information, such as using encrypted strings or secure credential stores. By integrating these security practices into database management scripts, IT professionals can protect critical data and comply with industry regulations. As organizations increasingly adopt automation and DevOps practices, mastering database connections in PowerShell becomes a vital component of a comprehensive network

©THE BOOK OF POWERSHELL
Copyrighted Material

@ISSO.TECH.ENTERPRISES

Copyrighted Material

management strategy, ultimately leading to enhanced efficiency and productivity in business operations.

Copyrighted Material
VICTOR P HENDERSON | ISSO-TECH ENTERPRISES™

CERTIFIED ETHICAL HACKER C|EH
ISSO-TECH PRESS™

Automating Database Tasks

Automating database tasks is a critical component for small businesses looking to optimize their operations and enhance efficiency. With the increasing reliance on data-driven decision-making, the ability to manage databases effectively is paramount. PowerShell, as a versatile scripting language, offers a powerful solution for automating routine database tasks such as backups, updates, and monitoring. This automation not only saves time but also minimizes the risk of human error, ensuring that database management is both reliable and efficient.

One of the primary advantages of using PowerShell for database automation is its ability to integrate seamlessly with various database management systems such as SQL Server, MySQL, and PostgreSQL. Through the use of built-in cmdlets and modules, IT professionals can quickly create scripts to perform repetitive tasks, such as executing SQL queries, managing user permissions, and scheduling regular backups. This functionality is especially beneficial for small businesses that may lack the resources for a dedicated database administrator. By empowering system administrators and network engineers to handle these tasks through automation, businesses can allocate their personnel to more strategic initiatives.

In addition to managing routine operations, PowerShell can play a crucial role in database monitoring and performance tuning. Automated scripts can be scheduled to run at regular intervals, providing real-time insights into database performance metrics, usage statistics, and potential issues. For instance, PowerShell can be used to monitor database growth and alert administrators when

©THE BOOK OF POWERSHELL
Copyrighted Material

@ISSO.TECH.ENTERPRISES

Copyrighted Material

thresholds are reached, enabling proactive management. This capability is vital for maintaining optimal performance and ensuring that database systems can scale with the growth of the business.

Security and compliance are also paramount considerations in database management, particularly for small businesses that must adhere to various regulatory standards. PowerShell enables administrators to automate security audits and compliance checks, ensuring that databases are configured correctly and that sensitive data is protected. Scripts can be developed to verify access controls, log activities, and generate compliance reports, reducing the manual effort required to maintain security posture. This automation not only enhances security but also provides peace of mind to business owners regarding their data management practices.

Finally, integrating PowerShell automation with cloud services such as Azure and AWS further expands the capabilities available to small businesses. With the increasing adoption of cloud technologies, the ability to manage cloud-based databases through automation is essential. PowerShell scripts can be utilized to automate tasks such as provisioning databases, scaling resources based on demand, and managing backups in the cloud environment. This integration not only streamlines operations but also supports the broader goals of digital transformation for small businesses, positioning them for success in a competitive landscape. By leveraging PowerShell for automating database tasks, small businesses can achieve greater efficiency, security, and scalability in their database management processes.

Copyrighted Material
VICTOR P HENDERSON | ISSO-TECH ENTERPRISES™

CERTIFIED ETHICAL HACKER C|EH
ISSO-TECH PRESS™

VICTOR P HENDERSON | ISSO-TECH ENTERPRISES™

CERTIFIED ETHICAL HACKER C|EH
Copyrighted Material

©**THE BOOK OF POWERSHELL**
Copyrighted Material

@**ISSO.TECH.ENTERPRISES**

Copyrighted Material

Security Considerations for Database Management

In the realm of database management, security considerations are paramount, especially for small businesses that may lack the extensive resources of larger enterprises. The sensitivity of data stored within databases necessitates a proactive approach to securing these environments. Small business owners, IT professionals, and system administrators must recognize that securing databases is not just a technical requirement but also a vital business imperative. The consequences of data breaches can be severe, impacting customer trust, legal compliance, and overall business viability.

One of the first steps in securing database systems is implementing robust authentication mechanisms. PowerShell provides a powerful toolset for managing user accounts and permissions within various database platforms. By automating the creation and management of user accounts through PowerShell scripts, administrators can ensure that only authorized personnel have access to sensitive data. This not only enhances security but also simplifies the management of user roles and responsibilities, allowing for a more organized and secure database environment.

Encryption is another critical component in safeguarding database information. Data at rest and in transit should be encrypted to protect against unauthorized access and data breaches. PowerShell can facilitate the implementation of encryption strategies by enabling administrators to automate the configuration of encryption settings for databases and connections. This includes

Copyrighted Material

VICTOR P HENDERSON | ISSO-TECH ENTERPRISES™

CERTIFIED ETHICAL HACKER C|EH
ISSO-TECH PRESS™

229.320.151.8

utilizing features such as Transparent Data Encryption (TDE) for SQL Server or configuring SSL connections for databases hosted in cloud environments. By integrating encryption into their database management practices, small businesses can significantly reduce the risk of data exposure.

Regularly updating and patching database systems is essential for maintaining security. Many vulnerabilities arise from outdated software, leaving databases exposed to potential threats. PowerShell scripts can automate the process of checking for updates and applying patches, ensuring that database systems remain up-to-date with the latest security enhancements. Additionally, implementing a regular backup strategy is crucial; PowerShell can be leveraged to automate backup processes, guaranteeing data integrity and availability in the event of a security incident or system failure.

Finally, continuous monitoring and auditing of database activity are vital to identifying and mitigating security threats. PowerShell can be utilized to create scripts that log and analyze database access patterns, providing insights into unusual or unauthorized activities. These monitoring practices not only help in compliance with regulatory requirements but also enable small businesses to proactively respond to potential security breaches. By adopting a comprehensive approach to database security, small businesses can safeguard their critical assets, enhance their operational resilience, and ultimately ensure their long-term success in a competitive landscape.

©THE BOOK OF POWERSHELL

Copyrighted Material

POWERSHELL

Copyrighted Material

VICTOR P HENDERSON | ISSO-TECH ENTERPRISES™

CERTIFIED ETHICAL HACKER C|EH

ISSO-TECH PRESS™

VICTOR P HENDERSON | ISSO-TECH ENTERPRISES™

CERTIFIED ETHICAL HACKER C|EH
Copyrighted Material

CHAPTER 10
DEVOPS INTEGRATION WITH POWERSHELL

©THE BOOK OF POWERSHELL
Copyrighted Material

@ISSO.TECH.ENTERPRISES

CHAPTER 10 | POWERSHELL DEV OPS INTERGRATION

PowerShell in CI/CD Pipelines

PowerShell has increasingly become a pivotal tool in the realm of Continuous Integration and Continuous Deployment (CI/CD) pipelines, particularly for small businesses aiming to streamline their IT processes. By leveraging PowerShell's robust scripting capabilities, organizations can automate tasks that traditionally required extensive manual intervention. This not only enhances efficiency but also reduces the risk of human error, which is critical for maintaining the integrity of deployments. For IT professionals and system administrators, integrating PowerShell into CI/CD workflows can lead to more reliable and repeatable processes, ultimately supporting business objectives through faster and more consistent application delivery.

One of the primary advantages of using PowerShell in CI/CD pipelines is its seamless integration with various development tools and platforms. PowerShell can interact with popular version control systems like Git, enabling automated checks and validations of code before it is merged into the main branch. Additionally, it supports various build servers such as Jenkins, Azure DevOps, and TeamCity, providing the flexibility to build, test, and deploy applications across different environments. This interoperability allows network engineers and system administrators to create custom scripts that can trigger builds, run tests, and deploy applications, ensuring that the entire process is cohesive and tailored to the specific needs of the business.

Copyrighted Material
VICTOR P HENDERSON | ISSO-TECH ENTERPRISES™

CERTIFIED ETHICAL HACKER C|EH
ISSO-TECH PRESS™

Security and compliance are paramount in any CI/CD process, and PowerShell offers robust features for managing these aspects effectively. By utilizing PowerShell scripts, organizations can enforce security policies, perform vulnerability assessments, and ensure compliance with industry standards throughout the deployment process. Automated security checks can be integrated into the pipeline to review code for potential vulnerabilities before it is pushed to production. This proactive approach not only enhances the overall security posture of the organization but also fosters a culture of compliance, which is particularly important for small businesses that may face scrutiny from regulatory bodies.

PowerShell also excels in managing cloud environments, which is increasingly relevant as more small businesses migrate to platforms like Azure and AWS. Automation scripts can be employed to provision resources, configure services, and manage deployments in the cloud, thus minimizing the time and effort required for these tasks. By incorporating PowerShell into cloud management practices, system administrators can ensure that cloud resources align with business needs, optimize costs, and maintain operational efficiency. This capability is especially beneficial for small businesses looking to leverage cloud technologies without overextending their IT resources.

In summary, the adoption of PowerShell in CI/CD pipelines presents a wealth of opportunities for small businesses, IT professionals, and network engineers. By automating routine tasks, enhancing security, and simplifying cloud management, PowerShell empowers organizations to streamline their development and deployment processes. As small businesses continue to navigate the complexities of today's technology

©THE BOOK OF POWERSHELL
Copyrighted Material

@ISSO.TECH.ENTERPRISES

Copyrighted Material

landscape, mastering PowerShell becomes an invaluable asset, enabling them to achieve operational excellence and remain competitive in their respective markets.

Copyrighted Material

VICTOR P HENDERSON | ISSO-TECH ENTERPRISES™

CERTIFIED ETHICAL HACKER C|EH
ISSO-TECH PRESS™

Managing Infrastructure as Code

Managing infrastructure as code (IaC) has become an essential practice for small businesses looking to optimize their IT operations and enhance scalability. By leveraging PowerShell, organizations can automate the provisioning, configuration, and management of their infrastructure, allowing IT professionals, system administrators, and network engineers to focus on higher-value tasks. IaC enables teams to maintain consistency across environments, reduce deployment times, and improve collaboration among stakeholders. This approach not only aligns with the principles of DevOps but also fosters a culture of continuous improvement and efficiency.

PowerShell provides a robust framework for implementing IaC through its extensive cmdlets and scripting capabilities. With tools like Desired State Configuration (DSC), administrators can define the desired state of their infrastructure declaratively. This means that rather than manually configuring servers or services, they can write scripts that describe the desired configuration. PowerShell DSC ensures that the infrastructure remains in the desired state, automatically correcting any deviations, thereby minimizing downtime and enhancing reliability. This level of automation is particularly beneficial for small businesses where resources may be limited, allowing them to maximize their operational efficiency.

Moreover, integration with cloud platforms such as Azure and AWS further amplifies the advantages of managing infrastructure as code. PowerShell's native support for these services enables IT professionals to automate cloud resource management seamlessly. Businesses can deploy virtual machines, configure networks, and

©**THE BOOK OF POWERSHELL**
Copyrighted Material

@**ISSO.TECH.ENTERPRISES**

Copyrighted Material

manage storage resources using PowerShell scripts, streamlining their cloud operations. This capability not only reduces the complexity of cloud management but also allows for rapid scaling, making it easier for small businesses to adapt to changing market demands and technological advancements.

Security and compliance are critical concerns for small businesses, particularly in an age where data breaches and cyber threats are prevalent. By implementing IaC with PowerShell, organizations can enforce security policies consistently across their infrastructure. Automated scripts can be used to audit configurations, apply security updates, and ensure compliance with industry regulations. This proactive approach minimizes vulnerabilities and enhances the overall security posture of the organization. Moreover, PowerShell's logging and monitoring capabilities provide valuable insights into infrastructure performance and security events, enabling IT professionals to respond swiftly to potential threats.

In conclusion, managing infrastructure as code using PowerShell offers small businesses numerous benefits, including increased efficiency, enhanced security, and improved scalability. By adopting this approach, organizations can streamline their IT operations and align with best practices in systems and network management. As businesses continue to evolve, the importance of IaC in facilitating agile and resilient IT practices will only grow, making it a vital strategy for small businesses aiming for success in today's competitive landscape. Embracing PowerShell for IaC not only empowers IT teams but also positions organizations to thrive in an increasingly digital world.

Copyrighted Material

VICTOR P HENDERSON | ISSO-TECH ENTERPRISES™

CERTIFIED ETHICAL HACKER C|EH

ISSO-TECH PRESS™

VICTOR P HENDERSON | ISSO-TECH ENTERPRISES™

CERTIFIED ETHICAL HACKER C|EH
Copyrighted Material

©**THE BOOK OF POWERSHELL**
Copyrighted Material

@ISSO.TECH.ENTERPRISES

Copyrighted Material

Collaboration and Version Control

Collaboration and version control are essential components in the realm of PowerShell scripting, especially for small businesses that rely on effective network management. In a landscape where IT professionals, system administrators, and network engineers often work in teams, the ability to collaborate efficiently while maintaining oversight of changes to scripts and configurations is crucial. Utilizing version control systems, such as Git, enables teams to track modifications, manage different versions of scripts, and revert to previous states when necessary. This practice not only enhances teamwork but also mitigates the risks associated with script errors or unintended changes.

The integration of version control into PowerShell scripting workflows allows for improved accountability and transparency among team members. By maintaining a history of changes, teams can easily identify who made specific alterations and the context in which those changes were implemented. This feature is particularly beneficial for small businesses, where resources may be limited, and the impact of errors can be significant. Additionally, clear documentation of script evolution supports knowledge sharing among team members, fostering an environment where best practices can be communicated and adopted more widely.

Collaboration through version control also facilitates smoother deployment processes. Many small businesses find themselves managing multiple environments, such as development, testing,

Copyrighted Material
VICTOR P HENDERSON | ISSO-TECH ENTERPRISES™

CERTIFIED ETHICAL HACKER C|EH
ISSO-TECH PRESS™

and production. With version control, scripts can be developed and tested in isolated environments before being merged into the main branch for production use. This staged approach decreases the likelihood of introducing bugs into live systems and provides a clear audit trail of changes made throughout the development lifecycle. Teams can leverage PowerShell's capabilities to automate deployment processes, ensuring that the right versions of scripts are executed in the correct environments.

Furthermore, version control systems can integrate with Continuous Integration/Continuous Deployment (CI/CD) pipelines, enhancing the DevOps practices of small businesses. By automating the testing and deployment of PowerShell scripts, organizations can accelerate their development cycles while maintaining high standards of quality and compliance. This integration enables system administrators and network engineers to implement changes rapidly and reliably, thus supporting the agility necessary for modern IT environments. The ability to roll back to previous versions of scripts ensures that any inadvertent issues can be quickly addressed, minimizing downtime and disruption.

Ultimately, the combination of collaboration and version control not only strengthens the efficacy of PowerShell scripting within small businesses but also aligns with broader strategic objectives. By adopting these practices, organizations can enhance their network management capabilities, streamline operations, and foster a culture of continuous improvement. As IT professionals and network engineers embrace these tools, they empower their teams to work more cohesively while ensuring that their PowerShell scripts are robust, compliant, and well-documented. In doing so,

Copyrighted Material

small businesses position themselves for success in an increasingly complex technological landscape.

Copyrighted Material

VICTOR P HENDERSON | ISSO-TECH ENTERPRISES™

CERTIFIED ETHICAL HACKER C|EH

ISSO-TECH PRESS™

VICTOR P HENDERSON | ISSO-TECH ENTERPRISES™

CERTIFIED ETHICAL HACKER C|EH
Copyrighted Material

CHAPTER 11
ADVANCED POWERSHELL TECHNIQUES

©THE BOOK OF POWERSHELL
Copyrighted Material

@ISSO.TECH.ENTERPRISES

Copyrighted Material

CHAPTER 11 | POWERSHELL ADVANCED TECHNIQUES
CUSTOM MODULES

Custom Modules and Advanced Functions

Custom modules and advanced functions in PowerShell represent a significant leap forward in the capability of small businesses to manage their network environments efficiently. By harnessing these features, IT professionals and system administrators can create tailored solutions that address specific business needs while also enhancing productivity and operational effectiveness. In this subchapter, we will explore the importance of custom modules and advanced functions, how they can be developed and utilized, and the best practices for implementation in a small business context.

Developing custom modules allows organizations to encapsulate functionality and streamline their scripts. This modular approach promotes code reusability, which is essential for small businesses that may not have extensive resources for ongoing development. By grouping related functions into a single module, IT professionals can simplify maintenance and updates. Additionally, custom modules can help standardize processes across the organization, ensuring that all team members are using the same tools and methods, thereby reducing errors and improving overall efficiency.

Advanced functions in PowerShell extend the capabilities of standard functions through features such as parameter validation, pipeline support, and advanced output processing. By

Copyrighted Material
VICTOR P HENDERSON | ISSO-TECH ENTERPRISES™

CERTIFIED ETHICAL HACKER C|EH
ISSO-TECH PRESS™

implementing these advanced functions, network engineers and system administrators can create more robust and user-friendly scripts that enhance automation and streamline workflows. For instance, using advanced parameter attributes can ensure that users provide the correct input, reducing the likelihood of runtime errors. Furthermore, functions that support the pipeline allow for seamless integration with other commands, enabling a more efficient and powerful command-line interface.

When integrating custom modules and advanced functions into daily operations, it is crucial to follow best practices to ensure maintainability and scalability. Documentation should accompany every module developed, outlining its purpose, usage, and any dependencies. This practice not only aids current users but also provides future IT professionals with the necessary context for effective management. Additionally, version control systems should be employed to track changes to modules over time, facilitating collaboration and minimizing the risk of introducing bugs during updates.

In conclusion, the strategic use of custom modules and advanced functions in PowerShell equips small businesses with the tools necessary for effective network management. By embracing these advanced scripting techniques, IT professionals can foster a culture of automation and efficiency that is critical in today's competitive landscape. As small businesses continue to evolve, the ability to create tailored solutions with PowerShell will be an invaluable asset, enabling them to adapt quickly to changing demands while maintaining a high standard of service and compliance.

©THE BOOK OF POWERSHELL
Copyrighted Material

@ISSO.TECH.ENTERPRISES

Copyrighted Material

Error Handling and Debugging

Error handling and debugging are critical components of effective PowerShell scripting, particularly for professionals managing network environments in small businesses. As network engineers and system administrators, the ability to identify, diagnose, and rectify issues swiftly can significantly impact both the efficiency of operations and the overall health of IT infrastructure. This subchapter delves into essential strategies for implementing robust error handling and debugging techniques within PowerShell scripts, ensuring that small businesses can maintain seamless network management and minimize downtime.

To begin, understanding PowerShell's built-in error handling mechanisms is paramount. The `$Error` automatic variable captures error records, providing insight into what went wrong during script execution. By leveraging `Try`, `Catch`, and `Finally` blocks, administrators can design scripts that not only handle exceptions gracefully but also allow for clean-up operations after errors occur. For instance, in a network management context, if a script fails to ping a device, the `Catch` block can be used to log the failure and notify the administrator without terminating the entire script. This approach fosters resilience in automated tasks, which is critical for maintaining service levels in small business environments.

Moreover, employing the `-ErrorAction` parameter can enhance error management within PowerShell commands. By specifying `Stop`, `Continue`, or `SilentlyContinue`, users can control how

Copyrighted Material
VICTOR P HENDERSON | ISSO-TECH ENTERPRISES™

CERTIFIED ETHICAL HACKER C|EH
ISSO-TECH PRESS™

229.320.151.8

errors are processed, allowing for more granular handling of exceptions. For instance, using `-ErrorAction Stop` can halt execution when a critical command fails, prompting immediate attention to the issue. This level of control is particularly beneficial in cloud management scenarios, where issues can cascade and impact multiple services. Equipped with these tools, IT professionals can ensure that their scripts respond appropriately to errors, preserving the integrity of the network.

Debugging is another essential skill in the PowerShell toolkit. The `Set-PSDebug` cmdlet provides a powerful mechanism for tracing script execution, enabling users to monitor variable values and command execution flow. By setting the debugging level to `1` or `2`, administrators can step through code, gaining insights into potential pitfalls. This is especially useful when developing scripts for tasks like database management or API integration, where understanding the interaction between components is vital for troubleshooting. Additionally, the use of `Write-Debug` and `Write-Verbose` cmdlets allows for the inclusion of detailed logging within scripts, providing context that can aid in diagnosing issues post-execution.

Finally, adopting best practices for logging and monitoring can further enhance error handling and debugging efforts. Implementing structured logging mechanisms, such as writing to a log file or sending logs to a centralized monitoring system, enables IT professionals to track script performance and error occurrences over time. This historical data can be invaluable for identifying recurring issues and trends, facilitating proactive maintenance and continuous improvement. Small businesses can leverage these

©THE BOOK OF POWERSHELL
Copyrighted Material

@ISSO.TECH.ENTERPRISES

Copyrighted Material

insights to refine their PowerShell strategies, ensuring that their network management operations remain resilient and efficient.

In conclusion, effective error handling and debugging practices in PowerShell are indispensable for small businesses aiming to optimize their IT operations. By mastering the built-in error management features, utilizing robust debugging tools, and implementing comprehensive logging strategies, network engineers and system administrators can significantly enhance their troubleshooting capabilities. Such proficiency not only minimizes downtime but also empowers small businesses to leverage automation confidently, driving productivity and success in an increasingly complex technological landscape.

Copyrighted Material
VICTOR P HENDERSON | ISSO-TECH ENTERPRISES™

CERTIFIED ETHICAL HACKER C|EH
ISSO-TECH PRESS™

Performance Optimization Tips

Performance Optimization Tips

In the realm of network management, performance optimization is crucial for ensuring that systems run efficiently and effectively. For small businesses, where resources may be limited, leveraging PowerShell can lead to significant improvements in operational workflows. By understanding and implementing specific optimization techniques, IT professionals, system administrators, and network engineers can enhance the performance of their PowerShell scripts and commands, ultimately resulting in better resource management and increased productivity.

One essential performance optimization tip is to minimize the use of unnecessary commands and loops within scripts. Each command executed in PowerShell incurs overhead, which can slow down performance, especially in scripts that run frequently or process large datasets. Instead of using multiple commands to achieve a task, consider using cmdlets that support pipeline processing. This reduces the number of individual operations and allows PowerShell to handle data more efficiently. Additionally, employing filters early in the command pipeline can significantly reduce the amount of data processed, leading to faster execution times.

Another effective strategy is to utilize background jobs for long-running processes. Instead of waiting for a command to complete, you can run it as a background job, freeing up your session for other tasks. This is particularly useful in environments where time is critical, such as cloud management scenarios involving Azure or

©THE BOOK OF POWERSHELL
Copyrighted Material

@ISSO.TECH.ENTERPRISES

Copyrighted Material

AWS. By offloading tasks to background jobs, system administrators can optimize their workflows, allowing for concurrent execution of multiple scripts or commands, thereby enhancing overall system performance and responsiveness.

Leveraging advanced features such as runspaces can also yield substantial performance benefits. Runspaces allow you to create multiple instances of PowerShell in parallel, which is particularly advantageous when executing tasks that can be distributed across different threads. For instance, in scenarios involving database management or API integration, utilizing runspaces can dramatically speed up operations by executing multiple queries or API calls simultaneously. This approach not only improves performance but also enhances the scalability of your scripts, making them adaptable to larger datasets or more complex tasks.

Lastly, regular performance monitoring and profiling of PowerShell scripts can reveal bottlenecks and inefficiencies. Using tools like Measure-Command to analyze execution time or the Get-Command cmdlet to review the performance of specific cmdlets can provide valuable insights into how scripts can be optimized further. By identifying and addressing slow-running components, IT professionals can fine-tune their PowerShell implementations, ensuring that they are not only effective but also efficient, ultimately leading to better system performance and smoother network management processes.

By adopting these performance optimization tips, small businesses can maximize the effectiveness of their PowerShell scripts and

Copyrighted Material
VICTOR P HENDERSON | ISSO-TECH ENTERPRISES™

CERTIFIED ETHICAL HACKER C|EH
ISSO-TECH PRESS™

commands. This not only enhances operational efficiency but also allows IT professionals and network engineers to focus on strategic initiatives that drive business growth. Embracing these techniques will empower organizations to harness the full potential of PowerShell, positioning them for success in the ever-evolving landscape of network management.

©THE BOOK OF POWERSHELL

Copyrighted Material

POWERSHELL

Copyrighted Material

VICTOR P HENDERSON | ISSO-TECH ENTERPRISES™

CERTIFIED ETHICAL HACKER C|EH

ISSO-TECH PRESS™

VICTOR P HENDERSON | ISSO-TECH ENTERPRISES™

CERTIFIED ETHICAL HACKER C|EH
Copyrighted Material

CHAPTER 12
BEST PRACTICES
NETWORK
MANAGEMENT

©THE BOOK OF POWERSHELL
Copyrighted Material

@ISSO.TECH.ENTERPRISES

Copyrighted Material

CHAPTER 12 | POWERSHELL BEST PRACTICES
NETWORK MANAGEMENT

Writing Readable and Maintainable Code

Writing readable and maintainable code is essential for small businesses that rely on PowerShell for various network management tasks. As IT professionals, system administrators, and network engineers, your scripts often become the backbone of your operations, automating critical functions and ensuring compliance with security standards. The clarity of your code not only facilitates troubleshooting and updates but also enhances collaboration among team members who may need to work with or modify your scripts in the future. Adopting best practices in coding can lead to significant time savings and reduced errors, thereby improving overall productivity.

One fundamental principle of writing readable code is the use of meaningful naming conventions for variables, functions, and modules. Names should accurately reflect the purpose and functionality of the code elements they represent. Instead of using generic names like `$var1` or `Function1`, opt for descriptive names such as `$userCount` or `Get-ActiveUsers`. This practice makes it easier for anyone reviewing the code to understand its intent without delving into the implementation details. Additionally, following a consistent naming convention across your scripts fosters a sense of familiarity, allowing team members to navigate your code with greater ease.

Copyrighted Material
VICTOR P HENDERSON | ISSO-TECH ENTERPRISES™

CERTIFIED ETHICAL HACKER C|EH
ISSO-TECH PRESS™

229.320.151.8

Incorporating comments and documentation within your scripts is another vital aspect of maintainable code. Comments should explain the rationale behind complex logic, outline the purpose of functions, and provide context for any significant decisions made during the coding process. While it may seem tedious to document every line, well-placed comments enable future developers—whether they are your colleagues or your future self—to quickly grasp the code's functionality without retracing the thought process. Furthermore, consider maintaining a separate documentation file or utilizing tools that generate documentation from your scripts, ensuring that your code's purpose and usage are always clear.

Structuring your code logically also enhances readability and maintainability. Organizing your scripts into functions or modules that encapsulate specific tasks promotes modularity, making it easier to test individual components without affecting the entire system. This modular approach allows for easier updates and debugging, as changes can be made to one part of the script without the risk of unintended consequences elsewhere. Additionally, using consistent formatting—such as indentation and spacing—helps to visually separate different sections of code, improving overall clarity.

Finally, embracing version control systems, such as Git, provides a robust framework for managing changes to your scripts. Version control not only keeps a history of modifications but also facilitates collaboration among team members. By tracking changes, you can easily identify when and where issues arise, roll back to previous versions if necessary, and maintain a clear audit trail for compliance purposes. Implementing these best practices will

©THE BOOK OF POWERSHELL
Copyrighted Material

@ISSO.TECH.ENTERPRISES

ensure that your PowerShell scripts remain readable, maintainable, and effective tools for network management, ultimately contributing to small business success.

Copyrighted Material
VICTOR P HENDERSON | ISSO-TECH ENTERPRISES™

CERTIFIED ETHICAL HACKER C|EH
ISSO-TECH PRESS™

Documentation and Commenting

In the realm of network management and system administration, effective documentation and commenting practices are crucial for ensuring the sustainability and scalability of PowerShell scripts. For small businesses, where resources may be limited, the ability to maintain clarity in code becomes even more essential. Well-documented scripts not only facilitate easier onboarding for new team members but also provide a straightforward reference for existing staff when revisiting projects. This chapter will delve into the strategies and best practices for documenting PowerShell scripts, emphasizing their significance in enhancing collaboration and maintaining operational efficiency.

The first step in effective documentation is to establish a consistent format for comments within your scripts. Comments serve as explanatory notes that describe the purpose of code blocks, the rationale behind specific commands, and any nuances associated with the script's functionality. For instance, incorporating header comments that outline the script's name, purpose, author details, and date of creation can provide immediate context for users. Additionally, inline comments should be used judiciously to clarify complex logic or to highlight critical decisions made during the scripting process. This level of clarity not only aids in troubleshooting but also minimizes the learning curve for individuals unfamiliar with a particular script.

In addition to comments, maintaining external documentation is equally important. This can take the form of user manuals, code repositories, or even a simple readme file accompanying your scripts. Such documentation should provide a comprehensive

©THE BOOK OF POWERSHELL
Copyrighted Material

④ISSO.TECH.ENTERPRISES

Copyrighted Material

overview of the script's functionality, usage examples, and any prerequisites needed for execution. For businesses leveraging PowerShell for cloud management or database management, detailed documentation ensures that stakeholders understand the implications of the scripts, especially when dealing with sensitive data or compliance requirements. Moreover, external documentation can serve as a vital resource during audits or security reviews, demonstrating adherence to best practices and compliance standards.

For IT professionals and network engineers, version control becomes an integral part of documentation. Utilizing tools like Git can help track changes made to scripts over time. This not only allows for accountability but also provides a historical record that can be invaluable when troubleshooting or rolling back to previous versions. By integrating version control into your documentation strategy, you can streamline collaboration among team members and ensure that all changes are well-documented. This practice aligns seamlessly with the principles of DevOps integration, where continuous improvement and collaboration are paramount.

Lastly, fostering a culture of documentation within your organization can significantly enhance the overall effectiveness of your PowerShell strategies. Encouraging team members to document their work not only normalizes the practice but also promotes knowledge sharing and collective problem-solving. Regularly scheduled reviews of documentation can ensure that it remains accurate and relevant, adapting to changes in technology or business processes. By prioritizing documentation and commenting, small businesses can build a robust foundation for

Copyrighted Material

VICTOR P HENDERSON | ISSO-TECH ENTERPRISES™

CERTIFIED ETHICAL HACKER C|EH
ISSO-TECH PRESS™

VICTOR P HENDERSON | ISSO-TECH ENTERPRISES™

CERTIFIED ETHICAL HACKER C|EH
Copyrighted Material

their PowerShell initiatives, ultimately leading to improved operational efficiency and success in network management.

©THE BOOK OF POWERSHELL
Copyrighted Material

④ISSO.TECH.ENTERPRISES

Continuous Learning and Community Resources

Continuous learning is an essential component for small businesses, IT professionals, system administrators, and network engineers who seek to master PowerShell and leverage its capabilities for effective network management. The technology landscape is ever-evolving, and staying updated with the latest features, best practices, and community insights can significantly enhance operational efficiency and service quality. Engaging in continuous learning not only enriches individual skill sets but also empowers teams to implement innovative solutions that drive business success.

One of the most effective ways to facilitate continuous learning is through community resources. These resources encompass a variety of platforms, including forums, online courses, webinars, and user groups dedicated to PowerShell. Websites such as GitHub, Stack Overflow, and PowerShell.org provide extensive repositories of scripts, troubleshooting tips, and collaborative projects where professionals can contribute and learn from one another. Participating in these communities fosters knowledge exchange and encourages practitioners to tackle real-world challenges collaboratively, thus enhancing their problem-solving capabilities.

In addition to online platforms, local meetups and user groups offer invaluable opportunities for networking and skill enhancement. Attending these gatherings allows professionals to connect with peers, share experiences, and discuss the latest

Copyrighted Material

advancements in PowerShell. Workshops and presentations from seasoned experts often provide insights into advanced techniques and practical applications tailored for specific niches, such as PowerShell for cloud management, security compliance, and DevOps integration. These interactions not only bolster technical skills but also build a support network that can be instrumental in navigating complex tasks and projects.

Furthermore, many educational institutions and training organizations offer certifications and specialized courses that focus on PowerShell and its applications in various domains. Pursuing these structured learning paths can lead to a deeper understanding of PowerShell scripting, automation, and integration with platforms like Azure and AWS. Such credentials not only validate expertise but also enhance professional credibility, making individuals more competitive in the job market and enabling businesses to attract skilled talent.

Ultimately, embracing continuous learning and utilizing community resources are pivotal for small businesses and IT professionals aiming to excel in network management with PowerShell. By actively seeking knowledge and engaging with the broader PowerShell community, organizations can foster an environment of innovation and adaptability. This commitment to learning not only drives operational excellence but also positions businesses to meet the challenges of an increasingly complex technological landscape, ensuring long-term success in their endeavors.

©THE BOOK OF POWERSHELL
Copyrighted Material

@ISSO.TECH.ENTERPRISES

©THE BOOK OF POWERSHELL

Copyrighted Material

PowerShell cmdlets along with a brief description of each:
1. Get-Command - Retrieves all commands available in PowerShell.
2. Get-Help - Displays help information for cmdlets and concepts.
3. Get-Alias - Retrieves aliases in the current session.
4. Get-ChildItem - Retrieves the child items (files and folders) in a specified location.
5. Set-Location - Changes the current location (similar to cd in cmd).
6. Get-Location - Retrieves the current location.
7. Clear-Host - Clears the display in the PowerShell console.
8. Get-Process - Retrieves information about processes running on the computer.
9. Stop-Process - Stops one or more processes.
10. Get-Service - Retrieves information about services on a computer.
11. Start-Service - Starts one or more services.
12. Stop-Service - Stops one or more services.
13. Restart-Service - Restarts one or more services.
14. Get-EventLog - Retrieves event log entries on the local or remote computers.
15. New-EventLog - Creates a new event log and a new event source on a local or remote computer.
16. Remove-EventLog - Deletes an event log and its configuration information on the local or remote computers.
17. Clear-EventLog - Deletes all entries from the specified event logs on the local or remote computers.
18. Get-WinEvent - Retrieves events from event logs and event traces on local and remote computers.
19. Clear-Variable - Deletes the value of a variable.
20. Get-Variable - Gets the values of variables.
21. Set-Variable - Sets the value of a variable.

Copyrighted Material
VICTOR P HENDERSON | ISSO-TECH ENTERPRISES™

CERTIFIED ETHICAL HACKER C|EH
ISSO-TECH PRESS™

22. Get-Content - Gets the content of a file.
23. Set-Content - Sets the content of a file.
24. Add-Content - Appends content to a file.
25. Get-Clipboard - Gets the current contents of the system clipboard.
26. Set-Clipboard - Sets the current contents of the system clipboard.
27. Get-Date - Gets the current date and time.
28. Get-Event - Gets events in the event queue.
29. Get-History - Gets a list of the commands entered during the current session.
30. Get-Item - Gets an item from a provider namespace.
31. Get-ItemProperty - Gets the properties of an item.
32. Get-Location - Gets information about the current working location.
33. Get-Process - Gets the processes that are running on the local computer or a remote computer.
34. Get-PSDrive - Gets drives in the current session.
35. Get-PSSession - Gets the PSSessions in the current session.
36. Get-Service - Gets the services on a local or remote computer.
37. Get-Variable - Gets the variables in the current console.
38. Get-WmiObject - Gets instances of WMI classes.
39. Invoke-Command - Runs commands on local and remote computers.
40. Invoke-Expression - Runs commands or expressions on the local computer.
41. Measure-Command - Measures the time it takes to run script blocks and cmdlets.
42. Measure-Object - Calculates the numeric properties of objects.
43. New-Object - Creates a new .NET object.
44. New-PSDrive - Creates a new drive in the PowerShell namespace.

©THE BOOK OF POWERSHELL
Copyrighted Material

@ISSO.TECH.ENTERPRISES

45. New-PSSession - Creates a new PSSession on a local or remote computer.
46. New-Service - Creates a new service.
47. Out-File - Sends output to a file.
48. Out-Null - Sends output to null, effectively discarding it.
49. Out-String - Converts input objects into strings.
50. Read-Host - Reads a line of input from the host console.
51. Receive-Job - Gets the results of background jobs.
52. Remove-Item - Deletes an item.
53. Remove-ItemProperty - Removes a property and its value from an item.
54. Remove-PSDrive - Deletes a drive from the session.
55. Remove-PSSession - Closes one or more PSSessions.
56. Remove-Service - Deletes a service.
57. Restart-Computer - Restarts the computer.
58. Restart-Service - Stops and then restarts one or more services.
59. Resume-Service - Resumes one or more suspended (paused) services.
60. Select-Object - Selects specified properties of an object or set of objects.
61. Select-String - Finds text in strings and files.
62. Set-Alias - Creates or changes an alias (alternate name) for a cmdlet or other command element.
63. Set-Content - Replaces the content of a file with new content.
64. Set-Item - Changes the value of an item to the value specified in the command.
65. Set-ItemProperty - Sets the value of a property of an item.
66. Set-Location - Changes the current location to the specified location.
67. Set-Service - Changes the properties of a service.

Copyrighted Material

VICTOR P HENDERSON | ISSO-TECH ENTERPRISES™

CERTIFIED ETHICAL HACKER C|EH
ISSO-TECH PRESS™

68. Set-Variable - Sets the value of a variable.
69. Show-Command - Displays a graphical command window.
70. Sort-Object - Sorts objects by property values.
71. Split-Path - Returns the parent portion of a path.
72. Start-Process - Starts one or more processes on the local computer.
73. Start-Service - Starts one or more stopped services.
74. Start-Sleep - Suspends the activity in a script or session for a specified period of time.
75. Start-Transcript - Starts a transcript of a command shell session.
76. Stop-Computer - Stops (shuts down) local and remote computers.
77. Stop-Process - Stops one or more running processes.
78. Stop-Service - Stops one or more running services.
79. Suspend-Service - Suspends (pauses) one or more services.
80. Tee-Object - Saves command output in a file or variable and also sends it down the pipeline.
81. Test-Connection - Tests network connectivity.
82. Test-Path - Determines whether all elements of a path exist.
83. Update-Help - Downloads and installs the newest help files for PowerShell cmdlets.
84. Wait-Event - Suspends the activity in a script or session until a particular event is detected.
85. Write-Debug - Writes debug messages to the debug stream.
86. Write-Error - Writes an object to the error stream.
87. Write-Host - Writes customized output to the host.
88. Write-Output - Sends the specified objects to the next command in the pipeline.
89. Write-Progress - Displays a progress bar within a Windows PowerShell command window.
90. Write-Verbose - Writes verbose messages to the verbose output.

©THE BOOK OF POWERSHELL
Copyrighted Material

@ISSO.TECH.ENTERPRISES

Copyrighted Material

91. Write-Warning - Writes a warning message to the pipeline.

92. Add-Computer - Adds the local computer to a domain or workgroup.

93. Add-Content - Adds content to the specified items, such as adding words to a file.

94. Add-PSSnapin - Adds one or more Windows PowerShell snap-ins to the current session.

95. Compare-Object - Compares two sets of objects.

96. Convert-Path - Converts a path from a Windows PowerShell path to a PowerShell Provider path.

97. ConvertTo-Csv - Converts .NET objects into a series of CSV strings.

98. ConvertTo-Html - Converts .NET objects into a series of HTML strings.

99. ConvertTo-Json - Converts objects to a JSON-formatted string.

100. ConvertTo-Xml - Converts objects to an XML-formatted string.

101. Copy-Item - Copies an item from one location to another.

102. Export-Alias - Exports information about currently defined aliases to a file.

103. Export-Clixml - Exports a .NET object to a CLIXML file.

104. Export-Csv - Converts objects into a series of CSV strings and saves them in a CSV file.

105. Export-FormatData - Saves formatting data from the current session to a file.

106. Export-PSSession - Imports commands from another session and saves them in a Windows PowerShell module.

107. Format-Custom - Formats the output as a customized table.

108. Format-Hex - Formats file content as hexadecimal values.

Copyrighted Material
VICTOR P HENDERSON | ISSO-TECH ENTERPRISES™

CERTIFIED ETHICAL HACKER C|EH
ISSO-TECH PRESS™

109. Format-List - Formats the output as a list of properties, each with its associated value.
110. Format-Table - Formats the output as a table.
111. Format-Wide - Formats objects as a wide table that displays only one property of each object.
112. Get-AuthenticodeSignature - Gets the signature objects associated with a file.
113. Get-Certificate - Gets certificates from a certificate store.
114. Get-Credential - Gets a credential object based on a user name and password.
115. Get-ExecutionPolicy - Gets the execution policies for the current session.
116. Get-HotFix - Gets hotfixes (also called patches) applied to the local computer.
117. Get-ItemProperty - Gets the properties of a specified item.
118. Get-Job - Gets the background jobs that are running in the current session.
119. Get-Process - Gets the processes that are running on the local computer or a remote computer.
120. Get-PSBreakpoint - Gets the breakpoints that are set in the current session.
121. Get-PSCallStack - Gets the current call stack.
122. Get-PSDrive - Gets drives in the current session.
123. Get-PSProvider - Gets information about the specified Windows PowerShell provider.
124. Get-Service - Gets the services on a local or remote computer.
125. Get-TraceSource - Gets the trace sources that are currently defined.
126. Get-UICulture - Gets the current user interface (UI) culture settings.
127. Import-Alias - Imports an alias list from a file.

©THE BOOK OF POWERSHELL
Copyrighted Material

@ISSO.TECH.ENTERPRISES

Copyrighted Material

128. Import-Clixml - Imports a CLIXML file and creates corresponding objects in PowerShell.
129. Import-Csv - Converts the CSV strings from a file into objects and stores them in a variable.
130. Import-LocalizedData - Imports language-specific data into the current session.
131. Import-PSSession - Imports commands from another session into the current session.
132. Invoke-Command - Runs commands on local and remote computers.
133. Invoke-History - Invokes a previously executed cmdlet or script block in the current session.
134. Invoke-Item - Invokes an executable or opens a file (or set of files) from the PowerShell session.
135. Join-Path - Combines a path and child-path into a single path.
136. Limit-EventLog - Sets the maximum size and retention policy for an event log.
137. Merge-Partition - Merges two adjacent free space extents into a contiguous extent.
138. Move-Item - Moves an item from one location to another.
139. New-Alias - Creates or changes an alias (alternate name) for a cmdlet or other command element.
140. New-Event - Creates a new event.
141. New-EventLog - Creates a new event log and a new event source on a local or remote computer.
142. New-Item - Creates a new item.
143. New-ItemProperty - Creates a new property of an item.
144. New-Module - Creates a new dynamic module that exists only in memory.
145. New-Object - Creates a new instance of a .NET object.

Copyrighted Material

VICTOR P HENDERSON | ISSO-TECH ENTERPRISES™

CERTIFIED ETHICAL HACKER C|EH
ISSO-TECH PRESS™

146. New-PSDrive - Creates a new Windows PowerShell drive.
147. New-Service - Creates a new service.
148. New-TimeSpan - Creates a TimeSpan object.
149. New-Variable - Creates a new variable.
150. Out-GridView - Displays tabular data in a grid view window.
151. Register-EngineEvent - Subscribes to events that are generated by the Windows PowerShell engine and by the events that are generated by the New-Event cmdlet.
152. Register-ObjectEvent - Subscribes to events that are generated by .NET objects.
153. Register-PSSessionConfiguration - Registers a PSSession configuration on the local computer.
154. Remove-Alias - Deletes an alias from the alias table.
155. Remove-Event - Deletes events from the event queue.
156. Remove-EventLog - Deletes an event log.
157. Remove-Item - Deletes the specified items.
158. Remove-ItemProperty - Deletes a property from an item.
159. Remove-Job - Deletes a background job.
160. Remove-Module - Removes modules from the current session.
161. Remove-PSSessionConfiguration - Removes a PSSession configuration from the local computer.
162. Remove-PSBreakpoint - Deletes breakpoints from the current session.
163. Remove-PSDrive - Deletes a Windows PowerShell drive.
164. Remove-Service - Deletes a service.
165. Remove-Variable - Deletes a variable and its value.
166. Rename-Item - Renames an item.
167. Rename-ItemProperty - Renames a property of an item.
168. Reset-ComputerMachinePassword - Resets the machine account password for the computer.
169. Restart-Computer - Restarts the computer.

©THE BOOK OF POWERSHELL
Copyrighted Material

@ISSO.TECH.ENTERPRISES

Copyrighted Material

170. Restore-Acl - Restores access control list (ACL) settings.

171. Resume-Service - Resumes a suspended (paused) service.

172. Save-Help - Saves help files in a specified format and location.

173. Select-Object - Selects specified properties of an object or set of objects.

174. Select-String - Finds text in strings and files.

175. Send-MailMessage - Sends an email message.

176. Set-Acl - Changes the security descriptor of a specified item, such as a file or registry key.

177. Set-Alias - Creates or changes an alias (alternate name) for a cmdlet or other command element.

178. Set-AuthenticodeSignature - Adds a digital signature to a file.

179. Set-Content - Replaces the content of a file with new content.

180. Set-Date - Sets the system time on the computer to a specified date and time.

181. Set-ExecutionPolicy - Sets the execution policies for the current session.

182. Set-Item - Changes the value of an item to the value specified in the command.

183. Set-ItemProperty - Sets the value of a property of an item.

184. Set-Location - Changes the current location to the specified location.

185. Set-Service - Changes the properties of a service.

186. Set-TraceSource - Sets the options for a trace source.

187. Show-Command - Displays a graphical command window.

188. Sort-Object - Sorts objects by property values.

189. Split-Path - Returns the parent portion of a path.

190. Start-Process - Starts one or more processes on the local computer.

191. Start-Service - Starts one or more stopped services.

Copyrighted Material

VICTOR P HENDERSON | ISSO-TECH ENTERPRISES™

CERTIFIED ETHICAL HACKER C|EH
ISSO-TECH PRESS™

229.320.151 8

192. Start-Sleep - Suspends the activity in a script or session for a specified period of time.
193. Start-Transcript - Starts a transcript of a command shell session.
194. Stop-Computer - Stops (shuts down) local and remote computers.
195. Stop-Job - Stops a background job.
196. Stop-Process - Stops one or more running processes.
197. Stop-Service - Stops one or more running services.
198. Suspend-Service - Suspends (pauses) one or more services.
199. Tee-Object - Saves command output in a file or variable and also sends it down the pipeline.
200. Test-Connection - Tests network connectivity.
This list covers a wide range of PowerShell cmdlets, from basic file and process management to advanced scripting and automation.

©THE BOOK OF POWERSHELL
Copyrighted Material

④ISSO.TECH.ENTERPRISES

©THE BOOK OF POWERSHELL

Copyrighted Material

POWERSHELL

Copyrighted Material

VICTOR P HENDERSON | ISSO-TECH ENTERPRISES™

CERTIFIED ETHICAL HACKER C|EH

ISSO-TECH PRESS™

VICTOR P HENDERSON | ISSO-TECH ENTERPRISES™

CERTIFIED ETHICAL HACKER C|EH
Copyrighted Material

CHAPTER 13
CASE STUDIES

©THE BOOK OF POWERSHELL
Copyrighted Material

@ISSO.TECH.ENTERPRISES

Copyrighted Material

CHAPTER 13 | CASE STUDIES
REAL WORLD APPLICATIONS

Success Stories from Small Businesses

Success stories from small businesses utilizing PowerShell illustrate the profound impact that effective scripting and automation can have on operational efficiency, security, and overall business growth. These narratives not only demonstrate the versatility of PowerShell as a tool but also highlight the strategic advantages that can be gained through its implementation. For small businesses, often operating with limited resources, the ability to streamline processes and enhance productivity can be a game changer in a competitive landscape.

One remarkable example comes from a small financial services firm that faced challenges in managing its extensive client database. With manual processes taking up valuable time and increasing the potential for error, the company's IT administrator decided to leverage PowerShell scripting for database management. By automating routine tasks such as data entry, report generation, and client communications, the firm significantly reduced processing times. This not only improved the accuracy of their data but also allowed the staff to focus on higher-value activities, ultimately leading to enhanced client satisfaction and retention.

Another success story is that of a small e-commerce business that struggled with network management and compliance. With

Copyrighted Material
VICTOR P HENDERSON | ISSO-TECH ENTERPRISES™

CERTIFIED ETHICAL HACKER C|EH
ISSO-TECH PRESS™

increasing concerns about data security and regulatory requirements, the company turned to PowerShell for its security and compliance needs. By utilizing PowerShell scripts to monitor network activity and enforce security policies, the IT team was able to proactively identify and mitigate potential threats. This approach not only strengthened the business's security posture but also ensured compliance with industry regulations, allowing the company to focus on growth without the looming fear of data breaches.

In the realm of cloud management, a small marketing agency successfully adopted PowerShell for integrating Azure resources into their workflow. Faced with the challenge of managing multiple cloud services, the agency's system administrator implemented PowerShell for automation, enabling seamless deployment and management of resources. By scripting repetitive tasks, the agency improved its operational efficiency and reduced cloud costs. As a result, the marketing team could allocate more time to creative strategies rather than technical challenges, driving better campaign outcomes and client satisfaction.

These success stories underscore the transformative power of PowerShell in small businesses across various sectors. By mastering PowerShell and employing it strategically, small businesses can not only streamline their operations but also ensure security and compliance, enhance collaboration, and ultimately position themselves for sustainable growth. As the demand for efficiency and agility in the business landscape intensifies, the adoption of PowerShell will continue to empower small businesses, enabling them to thrive in an increasingly competitive environment.

©THE BOOK OF POWERSHELL
Copyrighted Material

@ISSO.TECH.ENTERPRISES

©THE BOOK OF POWERSHELL

Copyrighted Material

Copyrighted Material

VICTOR P HENDERSON | ISSO-TECH ENTERPRISES™

CERTIFIED ETHICAL HACKER C|EH
ISSO-TECH PRESS™

Lessons Learned from Network Management Challenges

Lessons learned from network management challenges can provide invaluable insights for small businesses striving to optimize their IT infrastructure. The intricacies of managing networks often reveal gaps in knowledge and practices that, when addressed, can lead to significant improvements in efficiency and security. For small businesses, which typically operate with limited resources, understanding these lessons can mean the difference between operational success and costly downtime.

One of the key lessons learned is the importance of proactive monitoring and management. Small businesses often underestimate the value of maintaining a vigilant watch over their network performance. By implementing robust monitoring solutions through PowerShell scripts, IT professionals can identify potential issues before they escalate into major problems. This proactive approach not only minimizes downtime but also enhances the overall reliability of the network. Additionally, leveraging PowerShell's automation capabilities allows for routine checks and balances, freeing up IT staff to focus on higher-level strategic initiatives.

Another critical takeaway involves the necessity of thorough documentation and knowledge sharing. Network management challenges often arise from a lack of clarity regarding configurations, changes, and troubleshooting steps. Small businesses can benefit significantly from establishing comprehensive documentation practices. Using PowerShell to automate documentation processes ensures that network configurations and changes are recorded in real time. This practice

©THE BOOK OF POWERSHELL
Copyrighted Material

@ISSO.TECH.ENTERPRISES

Copyrighted Material

not only aids in current management but also serves as a valuable resource for onboarding new staff and addressing future issues more efficiently.

Security and compliance are also vital considerations that emerge from network management challenges. Small businesses frequently face threats that can compromise not only their data but also their reputation. By adopting PowerShell for security management, organizations can automate compliance checks and implement security best practices more effectively. This includes regular audits of user permissions, monitoring for unauthorized access, and ensuring that all systems are updated with the latest security patches. A proactive stance on security mitigates risks and fosters a culture of compliance within the organization.

Finally, integrating feedback loops into the network management process is essential for continuous improvement. Small businesses should regularly assess their network performance and gather input from IT staff and end-users alike. PowerShell can facilitate this by automating the collection and analysis of performance metrics, enabling organizations to make data-driven decisions. This iterative process of evaluation and adaptation ensures that network management strategies evolve in line with changing business needs and technological advancements, ultimately leading to a more resilient and agile IT environment. By learning from past challenges, small businesses can optimize their network management practices, paving the way for sustainable growth and success.

Copyrighted Material
VICTOR P HENDERSON | ISSO-TECH ENTERPRISES™

CERTIFIED ETHICAL HACKER C|EH
ISSO-TECH PRESS™

VICTOR P HENDERSON | ISSO-TECH ENTERPRISES™

CERTIFIED ETHICAL HACKER C|EH
Copyrighted Material

©THE BOOK OF POWERSHELL
Copyrighted Material

@ISSO.TECH.ENTERPRISES

©**THE BOOK OF POWERSHELL**

Copyrighted Material

Future Trends in PowerShell and Network Management

As we look toward the future of PowerShell and network management, several key trends are emerging that promise to reshape the landscape for small businesses, IT professionals, system administrators, and network engineers. The rise of cloud computing continues to drive the evolution of PowerShell, particularly as organizations increasingly leverage platforms like Azure and AWS for their infrastructure needs. The deep integration of PowerShell with these cloud services not only streamlines the management of resources but also enhances automation capabilities, allowing for the rapid provisioning and scaling of applications. This trend underscores the importance of mastering PowerShell as a tool for effective cloud management, enabling IT professionals to optimize workflows and improve service delivery.

Another significant trend is the growing emphasis on security and compliance in network management. As cyber threats become more sophisticated and regulatory requirements tighten, PowerShell is evolving to meet these challenges. Enhanced security features, such as Just Enough Administration (JEA) and Just-in-Time (JIT) access, are being integrated into PowerShell practices, allowing administrators to enforce stricter access controls and audit trails. For small businesses, this means that PowerShell not only becomes a tool for automation but also a critical component of their security strategy. By adopting these advanced features, organizations can protect their network environments while maintaining operational efficiency.

Copyrighted Material
VICTOR P HENDERSON | ISSO-TECH ENTERPRISES™

CERTIFIED ETHICAL HACKER C|EH
ISSO-TECH PRESS™

The integration of PowerShell within DevOps practices is another trend that is gaining momentum. As organizations adopt Agile methodologies and seek to foster collaboration between development and operations teams, PowerShell serves as a bridge that facilitates this integration. The ability to automate deployment processes and streamline continuous integration/continuous deployment (CI/CD) pipelines through PowerShell scripting enhances productivity and ensures that updates and changes are deployed seamlessly. For network engineers, mastering PowerShell in this context not only improves deployment efficiency but also contributes to a more resilient and responsive IT infrastructure.

Furthermore, the expansion of PowerShell's capabilities in database management and API integration is noteworthy. As businesses increasingly rely on data-driven decision-making, the ability to manage databases and interact with APIs using PowerShell becomes essential. Future trends indicate a growing need for PowerShell scripts that can automate data retrieval, manipulation, and reporting tasks, thereby enabling organizations to harness the power of their data effectively. This shift highlights the critical role that system administrators and IT professionals will play in mastering PowerShell techniques that facilitate database interactions and API integrations.

Lastly, the future of PowerShell and network management will see a heightened focus on user experience and troubleshooting. As networks become more complex, the need for advanced diagnostic and troubleshooting tools is paramount. PowerShell's capabilities in monitoring, logging, and real-time analysis will enhance IT support functions, allowing for quicker identification and

©THE BOOK OF POWERSHELL
Copyrighted Material

@ISSO.TECH.ENTERPRISES

Copyrighted Material

resolution of issues. By leveraging PowerShell's extensive libraries and community-driven modules, small businesses can equip their IT personnel with the necessary tools to ensure network reliability and performance. This emphasis on user-centric approaches will be vital as organizations strive to maintain a competitive edge in an increasingly digital marketplace.

Copyrighted Material

VICTOR P HENDERSON | ISSO-TECH ENTERPRISES™

CERTIFIED ETHICAL HACKER C|EH

ISSO-TECH PRESS™

VICTOR P HENDERSON | ISSO-TECH ENTERPRISES™

CERTIFIED ETHICAL HACKER C|EH
Copyrighted Material

THIS PAGE LEFT BLANK INTENTIONALLY!

©THE BOOK OF POWERSHELL
Copyrighted Material

@ISSO.TECH.ENTERPRISES

©THE BOOK OF POWERSHELL

Copyrighted Material

POWERSHELL

Copyrighted Material

VICTOR P HENDERSON | ISSO-TECH ENTERPRISES™

CERTIFIED ETHICAL HACKER C|EH

ISSO-TECH PRESS™

VICTOR P HENDERSON | ISSO-TECH ENTERPRISES™

CERTIFIED ETHICAL HACKER C|EH
Copyrighted Material

CHAPTER 14
CONCLUSION AND NEXT STEPS

©THE BOOK OF POWERSHELL
Copyrighted Material

@ISSO.TECH.ENTERPRISES

Copyrighted Material

CHAPTER 14 | CONCLUSION
NEXT STEPS

Recap of Key Concepts

In this subchapter, we will summarize the key concepts covered throughout the book "PowerShell for Network Management: Strategies for Small Business Success." This recap aims to reinforce the fundamental principles that small businesses, IT professionals, system administrators, and network engineers can leverage to enhance their operational efficiency and streamline network management processes. As we navigate through the complexities of network management, PowerShell emerges as an indispensable tool, providing the flexibility and automation necessary to meet the demands of modern IT environments.

One of the primary themes discussed is the mastery of PowerShell for system administration. The book emphasizes the importance of understanding the PowerShell environment, including cmdlets, modules, and scripts that form the backbone of effective system management. Mastering these components allows IT professionals to automate routine tasks, manage configurations, and deploy applications efficiently. By leveraging PowerShell's capabilities, administrators can significantly reduce the time spent on manual processes, thereby allowing them to focus on strategic initiatives that drive business growth.

In addition to foundational skills, the book delves into advanced PowerShell techniques and best practices, highlighting the

Copyrighted Material
VICTOR P HENDERSON | ISSO-TECH ENTERPRISES™

CERTIFIED ETHICAL HACKER C|EH
ISSO-TECH PRESS™

229.320.151.8

significance of scripting for automation. We explored how to create reusable scripts that can perform complex operations with minimal input. This approach not only enhances productivity but also promotes consistency across network management tasks. By automating routine processes, such as user account creation, system updates, and backup procedures, small businesses can minimize human error and improve overall system reliability.

The integration of PowerShell with cloud management platforms, including Azure and AWS, represents another critical area of focus. As small businesses increasingly adopt cloud services, understanding how to manage these environments using PowerShell becomes essential. The book outlines strategies for automating cloud resource deployment, monitoring, and security compliance. By harnessing PowerShell's capabilities in cloud management, organizations can optimize their resources, reduce operational costs, and ensure that their cloud environments are secure and compliant with industry standards.

Finally, the discussion on PowerShell's role in security and compliance underscores its importance in today's threat landscape. The ability to generate reports, monitor network activity, and automate security assessments is vital for any organization looking to safeguard its assets. By implementing PowerShell in security protocols, small businesses can establish robust compliance frameworks that not only protect sensitive data but also foster trust among stakeholders. This recap serves as a reminder of the transformative power of PowerShell when applied strategically within network management, ultimately positioning small businesses for success in an increasingly digital world.

©THE BOOK OF POWERSHELL
Copyrighted Material

@ISSO.TECH.ENTERPRISES

VICTOR P HENDERSON | ISSO-TECH ENTERPRISES™

CERTIFIED ETHICAL HACKER C|EH
Copyrighted Material

Resources for Further Learning

In the ever-evolving landscape of technology, continuous learning is essential for small businesses and IT professionals aiming to leverage PowerShell for network management effectively. This subchapter, "Resources for Further Learning," provides a curated selection of materials to deepen your understanding of PowerShell and enhance your skills in various niches, including automation, cloud management, security, and more. These resources range from online courses and books to community forums and official documentation, all designed to empower you in your professional journey.

One of the most valuable resources for mastering PowerShell is the Microsoft Official Documentation. This comprehensive guide offers detailed explanations, syntax references, and practical examples that cater to all skill levels. For those interested in specific applications, such as cloud management with Azure or AWS, the official documentation provides targeted insights and best practices. Additionally, Microsoft's learning platform includes free online courses tailored to various aspects of PowerShell, allowing users to progress at their own pace while gaining hands-on experience in real-world scenarios.

Books written by industry experts can also serve as an excellent resource for small businesses and IT professionals. Titles such as "Learn Windows PowerShell in a Month of Lunches" by Don Jones and "PowerShell in Action" by Bruce Payette offer structured learning paths that cover fundamental concepts and advanced techniques alike. These books often include practical exercises and real-world examples, making them ideal for system

©THE BOOK OF POWERSHELL
Copyrighted Material

@ISSO.TECH.ENTERPRISES

Copyrighted Material

administrators and network engineers looking to apply their knowledge directly to their work. Furthermore, exploring niche books focused on PowerShell for specific domains, such as security or DevOps integration, can help professionals tailor their learning to their immediate needs.

Engaging with online communities and forums can significantly enhance your learning experience. Platforms like Stack Overflow, PowerShell.org, and Reddit's r/PowerShell provide spaces for discussion, troubleshooting, and sharing best practices with peers and experts. Participating in these communities not only helps you resolve specific issues but also keeps you informed about the latest trends and techniques in PowerShell. Additionally, attending webinars and virtual meetups can offer insights from industry leaders and provide opportunities to network with other professionals who share your interests.

Lastly, consider exploring advanced training options such as certification programs dedicated to PowerShell and its applications. Certifications from recognized organizations can validate your skills and knowledge, making you a more valuable asset to your organization. Programs such as the Microsoft Certified: Azure Administrator Associate or Microsoft Certified: Security, Compliance, and Identity Fundamentals can complement your PowerShell expertise and enhance your career prospects. By continually investing in your education and skill development, you position yourself and your small business for long-term success in a competitive environment.

Copyrighted Material
VICTOR P HENDERSON | ISSO-TECH ENTERPRISES™

CERTIFIED ETHICAL HACKER C|EH
ISSO-TECH PRESS™

VICTOR P HENDERSON | ISSO-TECH ENTERPRISES™

CERTIFIED ETHICAL HACKER C|EH
Copyrighted Material

©THE BOOK OF POWERSHELL
Copyrighted Material

@ISSO.TECH.ENTERPRISES

Copyrighted Material

Encouragement for Implementation and Innovation

In the ever-evolving landscape of small business IT management, embracing innovative technologies is not just advantageous; it is essential for sustained success. For small businesses, the implementation of PowerShell can serve as a pivotal strategy that enhances operational efficiency and drives productivity. PowerShell is more than just a scripting language; it is a powerful tool that empowers IT professionals, system administrators, and network engineers to automate tasks, manage resources, and streamline processes. By fostering a culture of innovation through PowerShell, small businesses can not only optimize their existing workflows but also position themselves to adapt swiftly to new challenges and opportunities.

Implementing PowerShell solutions requires a mindset geared toward continuous improvement and exploration of new possibilities. Small businesses often operate with limited resources, making it crucial to leverage automation tools that can free up time and reduce human error. For IT professionals and network engineers, mastering PowerShell scripting can lead to significant improvements in operational efficiency. The ability to automate repetitive tasks—such as user account management, system updates, and network configurations—enables teams to focus on strategic initiatives that drive business growth. By embracing this approach, small businesses can cultivate a proactive environment that encourages the exploration of innovative solutions.

Copyrighted Material
VICTOR P HENDERSON | ISSO-TECH ENTERPRISES™

CERTIFIED ETHICAL HACKER C|EH
ISSO-TECH PRESS™

Moreover, the versatility of PowerShell extends beyond traditional IT management. It plays a vital role in cloud management, security compliance, and database administration, among other niches. Businesses leveraging platforms like Azure and AWS can benefit from PowerShell's seamless integration capabilities, allowing for efficient cloud resource management and orchestration. Encouraging team members to explore and implement these advanced features fosters a culture of technological innovation that can lead to improved service delivery and customer satisfaction. The proactive adoption of PowerShell in these areas not only enhances operational capabilities but also positions small businesses to compete more effectively in a digital marketplace.

Security and compliance are another critical aspect where PowerShell can make a significant impact. As cyber threats evolve, small businesses must prioritize robust security measures. PowerShell provides the tools necessary to automate compliance checks, monitor system health, and respond to security incidents in real time. By integrating PowerShell into their security frameworks, small businesses can enhance their resilience against potential threats, ensuring that they not only meet regulatory requirements but also build trust with their clients. Encouraging IT teams to innovate in this space not only safeguards the organization but also fosters a culture of accountability and responsibility.

In conclusion, the encouragement for implementation and innovation through PowerShell is vital for small businesses striving for success in a competitive environment. By investing in training and development, businesses can empower their teams to master PowerShell and harness its full potential. This commitment to innovation not only streamlines operations and enhances security but also drives a culture of continuous growth and adaptation. As small businesses embark on their journey with PowerShell, they do so with the confidence that they are equipped with the tools necessary to navigate the complexities of modern IT management.

Copyrighted Material
VICTOR P HENDERSON | ISSO-TECH ENTERPRISES™

CERTIFIED ETHICAL HACKER C|EH
ISSO-TECH PRESS™

VICTOR P HENDERSON | ISSO-TECH ENTERPRISES™

CERTIFIED ETHICAL HACKER C|EH
Copyrighted Material

©THE BOOK OF POWERSHELL
Copyrighted Material

@ISSO.TECH.ENTERPRISES

©THE BOOK OF POWERSHELL

Copyrighted Material

POWERSHELL

Copyrighted Material

VICTOR P HENDERSON | ISSO-TECH ENTERPRISES™

CERTIFIED ETHICAL HACKER C|EH

ISSO-TECH PRESS™

VICTOR P HENDERSON | ISSO-TECH ENTERPRISES™

CERTIFIED ETHICAL HACKER C|EH
Copyrighted Material

EPILOGUE

©THE BOOK OF POWERSHELL
Copyrighted Material

@ISSO.TECH.ENTERPRISES

Copyrighted Material

EPILOGUE | THE BOOK OF POWERSHELL
ISSO-TECH ENTERPRISES™

As we conclude ©*The Book of PowerShell*, it is important to recognize that PowerShell is more than just a tool—it is a gateway to mastering modern IT management, automation, and system administration. By understanding the core principles and leveraging the techniques outlined in this book, you have laid a strong foundation to streamline workflows, improve efficiency, and navigate the complexities of today's technology landscape.

The journey through PowerShell is one of continuous learning and adaptation. With its ever-evolving features, growing community, and cross-platform capabilities, PowerShell empowers you to stay ahead of the curve, ensuring that your skills remain relevant in an increasingly digital world. The command-line interface has become more than a utility—it is now a strategic asset that can transform the way you manage systems, solve problems, and optimize processes.

As technology advances, the need for automation, scalability, and secure management will only increase. PowerShell will continue to be an indispensable part of that evolution, enabling IT professionals, administrators, and developers to meet the demands of their environments with precision and confidence. The skills you've developed here can be applied in countless scenarios—from local system management to cloud automation—opening doors to greater opportunities and innovation.

Copyrighted Material
VICTOR P HENDERSON | ISSO-TECH ENTERPRISES™

CERTIFIED ETHICAL HACKER C|EH
ISSO-TECH PRESS™

VICTOR P HENDERSON | ISSO-TECH ENTERPRISES™

CERTIFIED ETHICAL HACKER C|EH
Copyrighted Material

Remember, mastering PowerShell is not the end of the road but a stepping stone. As you continue to explore and experiment, embrace the challenges that come your way. Stay curious, seek new knowledge, and build upon what you've learned. By doing so, you'll be well-equipped to adapt to emerging technologies, implement best practices, and contribute to the ongoing transformation of the IT world.

Thank you for embarking on this journey with *The Book of PowerShell*. Your dedication to honing your skills will not only benefit your career but also the broader technology community. Keep pushing the boundaries of what PowerShell can do—and let your success in automating and managing systems be a testament to the power of this incredible tool.

- VICTOR P HENDERSON -
CERTIFIED ETHICAL HACKER C|EH

©THE BOOK OF POWERSHELL
Copyrighted Material

@ISSO.TECH.ENTERPRISES

©THE BOOK OF POWERSHELL

Copyrighted Material

POWERSHELL

Copyrighted Material

VICTOR P HENDERSON | ISSO-TECH ENTERPRISES™

CERTIFIED ETHICAL HACKER C|EH

ISSO-TECH PRESS™

229.320.151 8

VICTOR P HENDERSON | ISSO-TECH ENTERPRISES™

CERTIFIED ETHICAL HACKER C|EH
Copyrighted Material

BIOGRAPHY

©THE BOOK OF POWERSHELL
Copyrighted Material

@ISSO.TECH.ENTERPRISES

BIOGRAPHY | VICTOR P HENDERSON
CERTIFIED ETHICAL HACKER | C|EH

Victor P. Henderson is a seasoned IT professional and a leading authority in the field of network and cyber security. With over 20 years of experience, he has navigated the rapidly evolving landscape of technology, consistently staying ahead of the curve. His expertise spans a wide range of areas, including ethical hacking, IT security engineering, and Cisco network management.

Henderson holds multiple professional IT certifications, a testament to his commitment to continuous learning and professional growth. He is a Certified Ethical Hacker, a credential that speaks volumes about his deep understanding of how to identify vulnerabilities and secure systems. As an IT Security Engineer, he has developed and implemented robust security protocols for numerous enterprise organizations. His role as a Cisco Network Professional has ushered him forward to architect, implement, and manage complex network infrastructures, further honing his skills in network security.

His book, "Defensive Ethical Hacking: Techniques, Strategies, and Defense Tactics", is a reflection of his extensive knowledge and experience. It serves as a comprehensive guide for IT professionals and enthusiasts, providing insights into the world of ethical hacking and network security.

Copyrighted Material
VICTOR P HENDERSON | ISSO-TECH ENTERPRISES™

CERTIFIED ETHICAL HACKER C|EH
ISSO-TECH PRESS™

VICTOR P HENDERSON | ISSO-TECH ENTERPRISES™

CERTIFIED ETHICAL HACKER C|EH
Copyrighted Material

Henderson's career is marked by a relentless pursuit of knowledge and a deep desire to help others navigate the complex world of IT security. His insights and strategies are invaluable to anyone looking to fortify their digital defenses. His commitment to his field and his passion for sharing his knowledge make him a respected figure in the IT community.

SOCIAL MEDIA: @ISSO.TECH.ENTERPRISES
WEBSITE: WWW.ISSOTECHENTERPRISES.COM

©THE BOOK OF POWERSHELL
Copyrighted Material

@ISSO.TECH.ENTERPRISES

©THE BOOK OF POWERSHELL

Copyrighted Material

POWERSHELL

Copyrighted Material

VICTOR P HENDERSON | ISSO-TECH ENTERPRISES™

CERTIFIED ETHICAL HACKER C|EH

ISSO-TECH PRESS™

VICTOR P HENDERSON | ISSO-TECH ENTERPRISES™

CERTIFIED ETHICAL HACKER C|EH
Copyrighted Material

ABOUT THE PUBLISHER

©THE BOOK OF POWERSHELL
Copyrighted Material

@ISSO.TECH.ENTERPRISES

©**THE BOOK OF POWERSHELL**

Copyrighted Material

ABOUT THE PUBLISHER | ISSO-TECH PRESS™, "Empowering Minds Through Innovative Information Technology Publishing"...

WEBSITE: https://WWW.ISSOTECHENTERPRISES.COM
SOCIAL MEDIA: @ISSO.TECH.ENTERPRISES

ISSO-TECH PRESS™, "Empowering Minds Through Innovative Information Technology Publishing"...

At ISSO-TECH PRESS™, we provide a platform for tech-savvy authors, writers, visionaries and innovators to fully express themselves and share their groundbreaking ideas. Our mission is to bring you the most insightful and transformative books in the world of information technology.

We empower experts to convey their knowledge and creativity, delivering profound and cutting-edge tech stories and insights. With

Copyrighted Material
VICTOR P HENDERSON | ISSO-TECH ENTERPRISES™

CERTIFIED ETHICAL HACKER C|EH
ISSO-TECH PRESS™

229.320.151.8

VICTOR P HENDERSON | ISSO-TECH ENTERPRISES™

CERTIFIED ETHICAL HACKER C|EH
Copyrighted Material

ISSO-TECH PRESS™, immerse yourself in the forefront of technological innovation and exploration.

***©THE BOOK OF POWERSHELL**
AUTOMATION, SCRIPTING, AND REMOTE IT MANAGEMENT FOR WINDOWS

***©CISCIO NETWORKS FOR NEW ENGINEERS**
TECHNIQUES STRATEGIES AND TACTICS

***©AI FOR SMALL BUSINESS**
ARTIFICIAL INTELLIGENCE HARNESSING AI FOR SMALL BUSINESS

***©DEFENSIVE ETHICAL HACKING**
TECHNIQUES STRATEGIES AND DEFENSE TACTICS

***©MASTERING ACTIVE DIRECTORY**
DIRECTORY SERVICES, SECURITY & INFRASTRUCTURE MANAGEMENT

©THE BOOK OF POWERSHELL
Copyrighted Material

@ISSO.TECH.ENTERPRISES

©THE BOOK OF POWERSHELL

Copyrighted Material

Designed by ISSO-TECH PRESS, set in Cinzel Decorative &
Times New Roman

Copyrighted Material
VICTOR P HENDERSON | ISSO-TECH ENTERPRISES™

CERTIFIED ETHICAL HACKER C|EH
ISSO-TECH PRESS™

229.320.151.8

VICTOR P HENDERSON | ISSO-TECH ENTERPRISES™

CERTIFIED ETHICAL HACKER C|EH
Copyrighted Material

©THE BOOK OF POWERSHELL
Copyrighted Material

@ISSO.TECH.ENTERPRISES

www.ingramcontent.com/pod-product-compliance
Lightning Source LLC
Chambersburg PA
CBHW070858160726
48004CB00003B/1133